THE DESIRE MAP PLANNER

from Danielle LaPorte

2019 DAILY

Danielle
LAPORTE

DANIELLELAPORTE.COM

- instagram.com/daniellelaporte
- daniellelaporte.com/facebook
- @daniellelaporte
- pinterest.com/daniellelaporte

The Desire Map Planner from Danielle LaPorte 2019 Daily Edition (Blue and Red)

Copyright © 2018 Danielle LaPorte Inc.
All rights reserved, Danielle LaPorte Inc.
ISBN: 978-0-9976514-8-5

Planner graphic design by Laurie Millotte, LaurieMillotte.com

Cover illustration by Marta Spendowska, VeryMarta.com

Printed and assembled in China, using natural soy bean inks, REACH certified foil and FSC-certified paper. Please recycle this planner. Mother Earth thanks you.

Post social pics of your Planner using **#DESIREMAP** so we can find you and show you some Love!

Hello Love,

This all started with one sticky note tucked into my agenda. I wrote down four feelings that I most wanted to experience that year—because when I sketched out my "goals" I wasn't all that lit up. But when I thought, *"Well, whatever I make happen I want to FEEL good about it,"* something shifted. I realized that it wasn't the particular achievement or "getting the thing" that was driving me. What I was going for was the *feeling I wanted to feel* when I got what I wanted (or thought I wanted).

I turned my ambition inside out. I got clear on my Core Desired Feelings. I put my goals and to-do's in service of my heart. And that sticky note turned into a book, a facilitator's program, and this planner collection. So there's something to this. And with every new Day Planner edition I say, *"This is even better than last year's."* But THIS is even better. After seven years, I think we've got this system dialed. To sum it up:

FEELINGS FIRST, then strategy. Because when you're clear on how you most want to feel, decisions happen more easily. You'll know when to say, *No, thank you,* and when it's a *YES!* From the micro tasks to the big stuff, this is about making more conscious choices.

I think a rich life is made of meaningfulness, and courage, and devotion to the sacred. A to-do list of obligations won't get you that. But some introspection and action just might. So this is where your heart meets your head and where your Soul directs your goals. I hope you light it up.

Here's to Love and flexible plans.

Put your Soul on the agenda.
love
Danielle

THE DESIRE MAP PLANNER *PROGRAM*

Welcome to **THE DESIRE MAP PLANNER PROGRAM**! Here's the arc of it: You start by investigating what's been working—and not working—in your life. Then you'll spot some patterns, notice some longings, get bummed out and super excited all at once, and you'll use those findings to declare your Core Desired Feelings. **Then you'll bridge those feelings to your intentions for the year.**

It's a simple methodology...but the way to clarity can be a bit messy. You have to get *in there*. Consider making uncomfortable changes. Think about incredibly sweet satisfaction. Fantasize about freedom. The objective is **clarity of feelings and direction**. We do this in 3 phases:

Free & Clear - Workbook 1
Your year-in-review. Reflect on what fuelled or drained you, what flopped and what soared. Take what you want forward and release the rest. This is a fun start.

Core Desired Feelings - Workbook 2
Knowing how you want to feel is the most potent form of clarity you can have. You'll identify 4 or 5 Core Desired Feelings to use as your planning guidance. This is poetic and deep.

Goals with Soul - Workbook 3
Rooted in your Core Desired Feelings, choose goals/intentions for the coming months. Goals with Soul, babe. This is strategy time.

Live it. Desire Mapping is an on-going practice. Here's how we support you…

The Planner Setup Guide
A digital guide with details about the Desire Map Planner Program so you can set up your planner and use it in a way that works for you.

Desire Map Weekly Planner Guidance
Weekly journal prompts and ideas for planning from your heart...your Core Desired Feelings.

Desire Map Monthly Planner Workbook
A monthly reflection exercise to reconnect with your intentions, and refresh or commune with your Core Desired Feelings.

Go here to download your workbooks:
DANIELLELAPORTE.COM/PLANNER-PROGRAM

HOW TO USE THE PROMPTS INSIDE THIS PLANNER:

MY CORE DESIRED FEELINGS
...write down how you most want to feel every day—all of your CDFs or just one in particular; the definition of the feeling, a promise to yourself, or some "ideas" about the feeling(s).

WHAT I WILL DO TO FEEL THE WAY I WANT TO FEEL
...what do you need to do, have, or experience for you to generate your Core Desired Feelings—your preferred states of being?

BODY & WELLNESS
...the key things you'll do to be well.

DEVOTION
...your spiritual practices. i.e. What/who will you pray for? Which meditations are you doing? Contemplation activities, rituals...what the sacred means to you.

NOT WORKING
...get real about the negatives so you can plan to transform them.

STOP DOING
...refer to your "NOT WORKING" notes and decide what needs to...stop.

GRATEFUL
...next to each gratitude, describe WHY you're grateful—it deepens the appreciation.

SOUL PROMPT
...open to interpretation. Just say what's in your heart.

REFLECT & ENVISION
...progress, pride. Delight and insight. Disappointment. Wisdom. Ideas.

*Work it, flow with it,
bend this planner to your will.*

ASTROLOGY OVERVIEW 2019

NEW MOONS
January 5 | Capricorn | 5:29pm*
February 4 | Aquarius | 1:04pm
March 6 | Pisces | 8:05am
April 5 | Aries | 1:52am
May 4 | Taurus | 3:47pm
June 3 | Gemini | 3:02am
July 2 | Cancer | 12:17am
July 31 | Leo | 7:12pm
August 30 | Virgo | 3:38am
September 28 | Libra | 11:27am
October 27 | Scorpio | 8:40pm
November 26 | Sagittarius | 7:07am
December 25 | Capricorn | 9:15pm

FULL MOONS
January 20 | Leo | 9:17pm
February 19 | Virgo | 7:53am
March 20 | Libra | 6:43pm
April 19 | Libra | 4:12am
May 18 | Scorpio | 2:11pm
June 17 | Sagittarius | 1:31am
July 16 | Capricorn | 2:39pm
August 15 | Aquarius | 5:31am
September 13 | Pisces | 9:35pm
October 13 | Aries | 2:10pm
November 12 | Taurus | 5:37am
December 11 | Gemini | 9:14pm

*All times in Pacific Standard Time (PST)

MERCURY RETROGRADES
March 5 - 28 | Pisces
July 7 - 31 | Leo - Cancer
October 31 - November 20 | Scorpio

ECLIPSES
January 5 | Partial Solar Eclipse | Capricorn
January 20 | Total Lunar Eclipse | Leo
July 2 | Total Solar Eclipse | Cancer
July 16 | Partial Lunar Eclipse | Capricorn
December 26 | Annular Solar Eclipse | Capricorn

ASTROLOGY GUIDE

ARIES
Cardinal Fire

Leadership.
Impulsive.
Takes action.

TAURUS
Fixed Earth

Sensualist.
Rooted.
Pleasure driven.

GEMINI
Mutable Air

Communicative.
Versatile.
Heady.

CANCER
Cardinal Water

Protective.
Nurturing.
Sympathetic.

LEO
Fixed Fire

Loyalty.
Sovereignty.
Generous.

VIRGO
Mutable Earth

Service-oriented.
Analytical.
Detailed.

LIBRA
Cardinal Air

Peacemaker.
Idealistic.
Craves balance.

SCORPIO
Fixed Water

Determined.
Alchemist.
Impassioned.

SAGITTARIUS
Mutable Fire

Philosophical.
Optimistic.
Positive.

CAPRICORN
Cardinal Earth

Wisdom.
Practical.
Thoughtful.

AQUARIUS
Fixed Air

Humanitarian.
Inventive.
Originality.

PISCES
Mutable Water

Empathetic.
Sensitive.
Imaginative.

FOUR ELEMENTS

Fire: Spirit
Earth: Matter
Air: Mind
Water: Emotion

THREE QUALITIES OF ASTRO ENERGIES:

Cardinal: Initiating
Fixed: Sustaining
Mutable: Dissolving

DESIRE. SOUL. GOALS.

If you've done the THE DESIRE MAP PLANNER PROGRAM, then you likely know:

- What you're bringing with you from your previous year and what you are so *done with* (Free & Clear - Workbook 1)
- Your Core Desired Feelings! (Workbook 2)
- Some clear intentions or goals, call them what you like, for the coming months (Goals With Soul - Workbook 3)

This page is where you record the highlights of all of the above to get your discoveries and declarations into one place—the sacred space of your Planner. Your CDFs and goals/intentions may change over the year. But start where you're at now and you can re-draft, erase, or add to this list as you go.

MY CORE DESIRED FEELINGS:

MY INTENTIONS & GOALS:

MY HABITS & RITUALS:

NOTES TO MY FUTURE SELF:

2019
overview

Focus + trust = space for magic to appear.

JANUARY

WK	M	T	W	T	F	S	S
01		1	2	3	4	5	6
02	7	8	9	10	11	12	13
03	14	15	16	17	18	19	20
04	21	22	23	24	25	26	27
05	28	29	30	31			

APRIL

WK	M	T	W	T	F	S	S
14	1	2	3	4	5	6	7
15	8	9	10	11	12	13	14
16	15	16	17	18	19	20	21
17	22	23	24	25	26	27	28
18	29	30					

JULY

WK	M	T	W	T	F	S	S
27	1	2	3	4	5	6	7
28	8	9	10	11	12	13	14
29	15	16	17	18	19	20	21
30	22	23	24	25	26	27	28
31	29	30	31				

OCTOBER

WK	M	T	W	T	F	S	S
40		1	2	3	4	5	6
41	7	8	9	10	11	12	13
42	14	15	16	17	18	19	20
43	21	22	23	24	25	26	27
44	28	29	30	31			

FEBRUARY

WK	M	T	W	T	F	S	S
05					1	2	3
06	4	5	6	7	8	9	10
07	11	12	13	14	15	16	17
08	18	19	20	21	22	23	24
09	25	26	27	28			

MARCH

WK	M	T	W	T	F	S	S
09					1	2	3
10	4	5	6	7	8	9	10
11	11	12	13	14	15	16	17
12	18	19	20	21	22	23	24
13	25	26	27	28	29	30	31

MAY

WK	M	T	W	T	F	S	S
18			1	2	3	4	5
19	6	7	8	9	10	11	12
20	13	14	15	16	17	18	19
21	20	21	22	23	24	25	26
22	27	28	29	30	31		

JUNE

WK	M	T	W	T	F	S	S
22						1	2
23	3	4	5	6	7	8	9
24	10	11	12	13	14	15	16
25	17	18	19	20	21	22	23
26	24	25	26	27	28	29	30

AUGUST

WK	M	T	W	T	F	S	S
31				1	2	3	4
32	5	6	7	8	9	10	11
33	12	13	14	15	16	17	18
34	19	20	21	22	23	24	25
35	26	27	28	29	30	31	

SEPTEMBER

WK	M	T	W	T	F	S	S
35							1
36	2	3	4	5	6	7	8
37	9	10	11	12	13	14	15
38	16	17	18	19	20	21	22
39	23	24	25	26	27	28	29
40	30						

NOVEMBER

WK	M	T	W	T	F	S	S
44					1	2	3
45	4	5	6	7	8	9	10
46	11	12	13	14	15	16	17
47	18	19	20	21	22	23	24
48	25	26	27	28	29	30	

DECEMBER

WK	M	T	W	T	F	S	S
48							1
49	2	3	4	5	6	7	8
50	9	10	11	12	13	14	15
51	16	17	18	19	20	21	22
52	23	24	25	26	27	28	29
1	30	31					

2020
overview

Strong preferences = deliberate creation.

_____
_____
_____
_____
_____
_____
_____
_____
_____
_____
_____
_____
_____
_____
_____
_____
_____
_____
_____

JANUARY

WK	M	T	W	T	F	S	S
01			1	2	3	4	5
02	6	7	8	9	10	11	12
03	13	14	15	16	17	18	19
04	20	21	22	23	24	25	26
05	27	28	29	30	31		

APRIL

WK	M	T	W	T	F	S	S
14			1	2	3	4	5
15	6	7	8	9	10	11	12
16	13	14	15	16	17	18	19
17	20	21	22	23	24	25	26
18	27	28	29	30			

JULY

WK	M	T	W	T	F	S	S
27			1	2	3	4	5
28	6	7	8	9	10	11	12
29	13	14	15	16	17	18	19
30	20	21	22	23	24	25	26
31	27	28	29	30	31		

OCTOBER

WK	M	T	W	T	F	S	S
40				1	2	3	4
41	5	6	7	8	9	10	11
42	12	13	14	15	16	17	18
43	19	20	21	22	23	24	25
44	26	27	28	29	30	31	

FEBRUARY

WK	M	T	W	T	F	S	S
05					1	2	
06	3	4	5	6	7	8	9
07	10	11	12	13	14	15	16
08	17	18	19	20	21	22	23
09	24	25	26	27	28	29	

MARCH

WK	M	T	W	T	F	S	S
09							1
10	2	3	4	5	6	7	8
11	9	10	11	12	13	14	15
12	16	17	18	19	20	21	22
13	23	24	25	26	27	28	29
14	30	31					

MAY

WK	M	T	W	T	F	S	S
18				1	2	3	
19	4	5	6	7	8	9	10
20	11	12	13	14	15	16	17
21	18	19	20	21	22	23	24
22	25	26	27	28	29	30	31

JUNE

WK	M	T	W	T	F	S	S
23	1	2	3	4	5	6	7
24	8	9	10	11	12	13	14
25	15	16	17	18	19	20	21
26	22	23	24	25	26	27	28
27	29	30					

AUGUST

WK	M	T	W	T	F	S	S
31						1	2
32	3	4	5	6	7	8	9
33	10	11	12	13	14	15	16
34	17	18	19	20	21	22	23
35	24	25	26	27	28	29	30
36	31						

SEPTEMBER

WK	M	T	W	T	F	S	S
36		1	2	3	4	5	6
37	7	8	9	10	11	12	13
38	14	15	16	17	18	19	20
39	21	22	23	24	25	26	27
40	28	29	30				

NOVEMBER

WK	M	T	W	T	F	S	S
44							1
45	2	3	4	5	6	7	8
46	9	10	11	12	13	14	15
47	16	17	18	19	20	21	22
48	23	24	25	26	27	28	29
49	30						

DECEMBER

WK	M	T	W	T	F	S	S
49		1	2	3	4	5	6
50	7	8	9	10	11	12	13
51	14	15	16	17	18	19	20
52	21	22	23	24	25	26	27
01	28	29	30	31			

JANUARY
2019

Bountiful am I.
Blissful am I.
Beautiful am I.

This is a mantra from Yogi Bhajan. You can speak or chant this out loud, as a whisper, or silently to yourself. Believe it.

MONDAY	TUESDAY	WEDNESDAY
WEEK 1	**New Year's Day** 1	2
Venus enters Sagittarius 7 **WEEK 2**	8	9
14 **WEEK 3**	**Makar Sankranti (Hindu)** 15	16
Martin Luther King, Jr. Day (US) 21 **WEEK 4**	22	Mercury enters Aquarius 23
28 **WEEK 5**	29	30

THURSDAY	FRIDAY	SATURDAY	SUNDAY
3	Mercury enters Capricorn 4	● New Moon in Capricorn - Partial Solar Eclipse 5	Uranus stations Direct in Aries 6
10	11	12	13
17	18	19	**Tu Bishvat / Tu B'Shevat Paush Purnima (Hindu)** 20 Sun enters Aquarius O Full Moon in Leo - Total Lunar Eclipse
24	25	**Australia Day** 26	27
31			

JANUARY

MONDAY December 31, 2018

MY CORE DESIRED FEELINGS

What I will do to feel the way I want to feel

SCHEDULE ... what do you really want to happen?

: _____
: _____
: _____
: _____
: _____
: _____
: _____
: _____
: _____
: _____
: _____
: _____
: _____
: _____
: _____
: _____

TO-DO ... imagine

1. _____
2. _____
3. _____
_____
_____

BODY & WELLNESS I will nourish my body ...

DEVOTION I will pray for (who/what) ...

NOT WORKING ... does it feel light or heavy?

STOP DOING ... speak up

GRATEFUL ... ask for more

Because ...

MAGICAL

Love yourself like it's your job.

TUESDAY January 1, 2019 | *New Year's Day*

MY CORE DESIRED FEELINGS   *What I will do to feel the way I want to feel*

SCHEDULE ... leave room for magic

: _____
: _____
: _____
: _____
: _____
: _____
: _____
: _____
: _____
: _____
: _____
: _____
: _____
: _____
: _____
: _____

TO-DO ... prioritize pleasure

1. _____
2. _____
3. _____
_____
_____
_____

BODY & WELLNESS My body helps me ...

DEVOTION My meditation will be ...

NOT WORKING ... name it so you can change it

STOP DOING ... *No* makes way for *Yes*

GRATEFUL ... gratitude puts everything into perspective   *Because ...*

Only you need to trust your intuition.

KINDRED

WEDNESDAY January 2, 2019

MY CORE DESIRED FEELINGS

What I will do to feel the way I want to feel

SCHEDULE ... work for Love

: _____
: _____
: _____
: _____
: _____
: _____
: _____
: _____
: _____
: _____
: _____
: _____
: _____
: _____
: _____
: _____

TO-DO ... do what lights you up

1. _____
2. _____
3. _____
   _____
   _____
   _____

BODY & WELLNESS My body is ...

DEVOTION I will dedicate this day to ...

NOT WORKING ... don't hold back

STOP DOING ... clarity is power

GRATEFUL ... note WHY you're grateful

Because ...

LIGHT

The sacred flourishes with respect.

THURSDAY January 3, 2019

MY CORE DESIRED FEELINGS   *What I will do to feel the way I want to feel*

SCHEDULE ... simplicity is freedom

: _____
: _____
: _____
: _____
: _____
: _____
: _____
: _____
: _____
: _____
: _____
: _____
: _____
: _____
: _____
: _____
: _____

TO-DO ... believe in yourself

1. _____
2. _____
3. _____
_____
_____
_____

BODY & WELLNESS My body is telling me ...

DEVOTION I will light a candle for ...

NOT WORKING ... claim it. Tame it.

STOP DOING ... don't take any crap

GRATEFUL ... be a beacon of optimism   *Because ...*

MINDFUL

How you listen is how you live.

FRIDAY January 4, 2019 | *Mercury enters Capricorn*

MY CORE DESIRED FEELINGS   *What I will do to feel the way I want to feel*

SCHEDULE ... does it light you up?

: _____
: _____
: _____
: _____
: _____
: _____
: _____
: _____
: _____
: _____
: _____
: _____
: _____
: _____
: _____

TO-DO ... clarity creates simplicity

1. _____
2. _____
3. _____
   _____
   _____
   _____

BODY & WELLNESS I will respect my body ...

DEVOTION I will have faith that ...

NOT WORKING ... feel free

STOP DOING ... freedom is your birthright

GRATEFUL ... specificity intensifies gratitude   *Because ...*

HELPFUL

The universe has an excellent imagination.

SATURDAY January 5, 2019
● *New Moon in Capricorn - Partial Solar Eclipse*

MY CORE DESIRED FEELINGS

TO-DO ... let it be easy

1. _____
2. _____
3. _____
   _____
   _____
   _____

REFLECT
What Core Desired Feeling felt most alive in your life? Why/how?

SUNDAY January 6, 2019
Uranus stations Direct in Aries

What I will do to feel the way I want to feel

TO-DO ... make space for the light to enter

1. _____
2. _____
3. _____
   _____
   _____
   _____

ENVISION
What rituals support your Core Desired Feelings?

SOUL PROMPT I choose

Love flows when you relax.

FIERCELY

MONDAY January 7, 2019 | *Venus enters Sagittarius*

MY CORE DESIRED FEELINGS

What I will do to feel the way I want to feel

SCHEDULE ... joy expands time

: _____
: _____
: _____
: _____
: _____
: _____
: _____
: _____
: _____
: _____
: _____
: _____
: _____
: _____
: _____
: _____

TO-DO ... keep your soul on the agenda

1. _____
2. _____
3. _____
   _____
   _____
   _____

BODY & WELLNESS My body knows ...

DEVOTION Devotion creates miracles.

NOT WORKING ... does it feel light or heavy?

STOP DOING ... speak up

GRATEFUL ... ask for more

Because ...

FEMININE

Trust is a milestone.

TUESDAY January 8, 2019

MY CORE DESIRED FEELINGS   *What I will do to feel the way I want to feel*

SCHEDULE ... take up space

: _____
: _____
: _____
: _____
: _____
: _____
: _____
: _____
: _____
: _____
: _____
: _____
: _____
: _____
: _____
: _____

TO-DO ... make choices that liberate you

1. _____
2. _____
3. _____
   _____
   _____
   _____

BODY & WELLNESS I will tend to my body ...

DEVOTION I will contemplate ...

NOT WORKING ... name it so you can change it

STOP DOING ... *No* makes way for *Yes*

GRATEFUL ... gratitude puts everything into perspective   *Because ...*

A sure way to keep your ego in check is to intend to be as useful as possible.

SPIRITED

WEDNESDAY January 9, 2019

MY CORE DESIRED FEELINGS

What I will do to feel the way I want to feel

SCHEDULE ... what do you really want to happen?

: _____
: _____
: _____
: _____
: _____
: _____
: _____
: _____
: _____
: _____
: _____
: _____
: _____
: _____
: _____
: _____

TO-DO ... imagine

1. _____
2. _____
3. _____
   _____
   _____
   _____

BODY & WELLNESS I will nourish my body ...

DEVOTION I will pray for (who/what) ...

NOT WORKING ... don't hold back

STOP DOING ... clarity is power

GRATEFUL ... note WHY you're grateful

Because ...

OPENNESS

Enthusiasm is a heightened state of consciousness.

THURSDAY January 10, 2019

MY CORE DESIRED FEELINGS

What I will do to feel the way I want to feel

SCHEDULE ... leave room for magic

: _____
: _____
: _____
: _____
: _____
: _____
: _____
: _____
: _____
: _____
: _____
: _____
: _____
: _____
: _____
: _____
: _____

TO-DO ... prioritize pleasure

1. _____
2. _____
3. _____
   _____
   _____
   _____

BODY & WELLNESS My body helps me ...

DEVOTION My meditation will be ...

NOT WORKING ... claim it. Tame it.

STOP DOING ... don't take any crap

GRATEFUL ... be a beacon of optimism

Because ...

According to who? According to YOU.

WARMTH

FRIDAY January 11, 2019

MY CORE DESIRED FEELINGS

What I will do to feel the way I want to feel

SCHEDULE ... work for Love

: _____
: _____
: _____
: _____
: _____
: _____
: _____
: _____
: _____
: _____
: _____
: _____
: _____
: _____
: _____
: _____

TO-DO ... do what lights you up

1. _____
2. _____
3. _____
   _____
   _____

BODY & WELLNESS My body is ...

DEVOTION I will dedicate this day to ...

NOT WORKING ... feel free

STOP DOING ... freedom is your birthright

GRATEFUL ... specificity intensifies gratitude

Because ...

EXCITED

Let the healing begin.

SATURDAY January 12, 2019

MY CORE DESIRED FEELINGS

TO-DO ... what would be comforting?

1. _____
2. _____
3. _____

_____
_____
_____

REFLECT
Which Core Desired Feeling seems farthest away? How do you feel about that?

SOUL PROMPT I'm embracing

SUNDAY January 13, 2019

What I will do to feel the way I want to feel

TO-DO ... relax ... rebel ... rest

1. _____
2. _____
3. _____

_____
_____
_____

ENVISION
What would help you feel your Core Desired Feelings this week?

True intimacy trumps technique.

INVIGORATED

MONDAY January 14, 2019

MY CORE DESIRED FEELINGS

What I will do to feel the way I want to feel

SCHEDULE ... simplicity is freedom

- : _____
- : _____
- : _____
- : _____
- : _____
- : _____
- : _____
- : _____
- : _____
- : _____
- : _____
- : _____
- : _____
- : _____
- : _____
- : _____
- : _____

TO-DO ... believe in yourself

1. _____
2. _____
3. _____
   _____
   _____

BODY & WELLNESS My body is telling me ...

DEVOTION I will light a candle for ...

NOT WORKING ... does it feel light or heavy?

STOP DOING ... speak up

GRATEFUL ... ask for more

Because ...

SELFLESS

Your pleasure enlightens other people.

TUESDAY January 15, 2019 | *Makar Sankranti (Hindu)*

MY CORE DESIRED FEELINGS   *What I will do to feel the way I want to feel*

SCHEDULE ... does it light you up?

: _____
: _____
: _____
: _____
: _____
: _____
: _____
: _____
: _____
: _____
: _____
: _____
: _____
: _____
: _____
: _____

TO-DO ... clarity creates simplicity

1. _____
2. _____
3. _____
   _____
   _____
   _____

BODY & WELLNESS I will respect my body ...

DEVOTION I will have faith that ...

NOT WORKING ... name it so you can change it

STOP DOING ... *No* makes way for *Yes*

GRATEFUL ... gratitude puts everything into perspective   *Because ...*

VISIBLE

You don't need to know the answer before you begin.

WEDNESDAY January 16, 2019

MY CORE DESIRED FEELINGS

What I will do to feel the way I want to feel

SCHEDULE ... joy expands time

: _____
: _____
: _____
: _____
: _____
: _____
: _____
: _____
: _____
: _____
: _____
: _____
: _____
: _____
: _____
: _____

TO-DO ... keep your soul on the agenda

1. _____
2. _____
3. _____
   _____
   _____
   _____

BODY & WELLNESS My body knows ...

DEVOTION Devotion creates miracles.

NOT WORKING ... don't hold back

STOP DOING ... clarity is power

GRATEFUL ... note WHY you're grateful

Because ...

INTRIGUING

Negative feelings are wake up calls.

THURSDAY January 17, 2019

MY CORE DESIRED FEELINGS

What I will do to feel the way I want to feel

SCHEDULE ... take up space

: _____
: _____
: _____
: _____
: _____
: _____
: _____
: _____
: _____
: _____
: _____
: _____
: _____
: _____
: _____
: _____
: _____

TO-DO ... make choices that liberate you

1. _____
2. _____
3. _____
   _____
   _____
   _____

BODY & WELLNESS I will tend to my body ...

DEVOTION I will contemplate ...

NOT WORKING ... claim it. Tame it.

STOP DOING ... don't take any crap

GRATEFUL ... be a beacon of optimism

Because ...

SIMPLICITY

Stand up for yourself. (Some people will take this personally. It's okay.)

FRIDAY January 18, 2019

MY CORE DESIRED FEELINGS

What I will do to feel the way I want to feel

SCHEDULE ... what do you really want to happen?

: _____
: _____
: _____
: _____
: _____
: _____
: _____
: _____
: _____
: _____
: _____
: _____
: _____
: _____
: _____
: _____

TO-DO ... imagine

1. _____
2. _____
3. _____
_____
_____
_____

BODY & WELLNESS I will nourish my body ...

DEVOTION I will pray for (who/what) ...

NOT WORKING ... feel free

STOP DOING ... freedom is your birthright

GRATEFUL ... specificity intensifies gratitude

Because ...

BOUNTIFUL

It's all about the why.

SATURDAY January 19, 2019

MY CORE DESIRED FEELINGS

SUNDAY January 20, 2019

Tu Bishvat / Tu B'Shevat (Jewish holiday)
Paush Purnima (Hindu)
Sun enters Aquarius | ○ Full Moon in Leo - Total Lunar Eclipse

What I will do to feel the way I want to feel

TO-DO ... visualize your ideal life

1. _____
2. _____
3. _____
_____
_____
_____

TO-DO ... let it be easy

1. _____
2. _____
3. _____
_____
_____
_____

REFLECT
When you are feeling your CDFs, how does that help you be of more service to others?

ENVISION
How will you show up in the world as one of your CDFs?

SOUL PROMPT I don't want to

What if nothing changed?

PERSEVERANCE

MONDAY January 21, 2019 | *Martin Luther King, Jr. Day (US)*

MY CORE DESIRED FEELINGS

What I will do to feel the way I want to feel

SCHEDULE ... leave room for magic

: _____
: _____
: _____
: _____
: _____
: _____
: _____
: _____
: _____
: _____
: _____
: _____
: _____
: _____
: _____
: _____

TO-DO ... prioritize pleasure

1. _____
2. _____
3. _____
   _____
   _____
   _____

BODY & WELLNESS My body helps me ...

DEVOTION My meditation will be ...

NOT WORKING ... does it feel light or heavy?

STOP DOING ... speak up

GRATEFUL ... ask for more

Because ...

IN LOVE

Shatter the legacy that's holding you back.

TUESDAY January 22, 2019

MY CORE DESIRED FEELINGS

What I will do to feel the way I want to feel

SCHEDULE ... work for Love

: _____
: _____
: _____
: _____
: _____
: _____
: _____
: _____
: _____
: _____
: _____
: _____
: _____
: _____
: _____
: _____

TO-DO ... do what lights you up

1. _____
2. _____
3. _____
   _____
   _____
   _____

BODY & WELLNESS My body is ...

DEVOTION I will dedicate this day to ...

NOT WORKING ... name it so you can change it

STOP DOING ... *No* makes way for *Yes*

GRATEFUL ... gratitude puts everything into perspective

Because ...

Know what you're afraid of.

WORTHY

WEDNESDAY January 23, 2019 | *Mercury enters Aquarius*

MY CORE DESIRED FEELINGS   *What I will do to feel the way I want to feel*

SCHEDULE ... simplicity is freedom

: _____
: _____
: _____
: _____
: _____
: _____
: _____
: _____
: _____
: _____
: _____
: _____
: _____
: _____
: _____

TO-DO ... believe in yourself

1. _____
2. _____
3. _____
    _____
    _____

BODY & WELLNESS My body is telling me ...

DEVOTION I will light a candle for ...

NOT WORKING ... don't hold back

STOP DOING ... clarity is power

GRATEFUL ... note WHY you're grateful   *Because ...*

TRUST

Betrayal is an initiation.

# THURSDAY January 24, 2019

MY CORE DESIRED FEELINGS   *What I will do to feel the way I want to feel*

SCHEDULE ... does it light you up?   **TO-DO** ... clarity creates simplicity

: _____   1. _____
: _____   2. _____
: _____   3. _____
: _____   _____
: _____   _____
: _____   _____
: _____
: _____   **BODY & WELLNESS** I will respect my body ...
: _____
: _____   **DEVOTION** I will have faith that ...
: _____
: _____
: _____   **NOT WORKING** ... claim it. Tame it.
: _____
: _____
: _____   **STOP DOING** ... don't take any crap
: _____
: _____

GRATEFUL ... be a beacon of optimism   *Because ...*

SIGNIFICANT

Boundaries are the parent of creativity.

FRIDAY January 25, 2019

MY CORE DESIRED FEELINGS

What I will do to feel the way I want to feel

SCHEDULE ... joy expands time

: _____
: _____
: _____
: _____
: _____
: _____
: _____
: _____
: _____
: _____
: _____
: _____
: _____
: _____
: _____
: _____

TO-DO ... keep your soul on the agenda

1. _____
2. _____
3. _____
   _____
   _____
   _____

BODY & WELLNESS My body knows ...

DEVOTION Devotion creates miracles.

NOT WORKING ... feel free

STOP DOING ... freedom is your birthright

GRATEFUL ... specificity intensifies gratitude

Because ...

DIVINE GRACE

Every time you stand up to the dark you get lighter.

SATURDAY January 26, 2019
Australia Day

MY CORE DESIRED FEELINGS

TO-DO ... make space for the light to enter

1. _____
2. _____
3. _____
_____
_____
_____

REFLECT
Have a conversation with one of your CDFs, ask it to give you some guidance.

SUNDAY January 27, 2019

What I will do to feel the way I want to feel

TO-DO ... what would be comforting?

1. _____
2. _____
3. _____
_____
_____
_____

ENVISION
What spaces or places embody your Core Desired Feelings?

SOUL PROMPT The most encouraging thing someone could say to you right now would be

Refuse to go numb.

REALIZED

MONDAY January 28, 2019

MY CORE DESIRED FEELINGS   *What I will do to feel the way I want to feel*

SCHEDULE ... take up space

: _____
: _____
: _____
: _____
: _____
: _____
: _____
: _____
: _____
: _____
: _____
: _____
: _____
: _____
: _____
: _____

TO-DO ... make choices that liberate you

1. _____
2. _____
3. _____
    _____
    _____
    _____

BODY & WELLNESS I will tend to my body ...

DEVOTION I will contemplate ...

NOT WORKING ... does it feel light or heavy?

STOP DOING ... speak up

GRATEFUL ... ask for more   *Because ...*

BUOYANT

You will cash in on your good karma when the time is right.

TUESDAY January 29, 2019

MY CORE DESIRED FEELINGS

What I will do to feel the way I want to feel

SCHEDULE ... what do you really want to happen?

: _____
: _____
: _____
: _____
: _____
: _____
: _____
: _____
: _____
: _____
: _____
: _____
: _____
: _____
: _____
: _____
: _____

TO-DO ... imagine

1. _____
2. _____
3. _____
   _____
   _____
   _____

BODY & WELLNESS I will nourish my body ...

DEVOTION I will pray for (who/what) ...

NOT WORKING ... name it so you can change it

STOP DOING ... *No* makes way for *Yes*

GRATEFUL ... gratitude puts everything into perspective

Because ...

FREEDOM

Attend first to the divine and the work at hand becomes art.

WEDNESDAY January 30, 2019

MY CORE DESIRED FEELINGS

What I will do to feel the way I want to feel

SCHEDULE ... leave room for magic

: _____
: _____
: _____
: _____
: _____
: _____
: _____
: _____
: _____
: _____
: _____
: _____
: _____
: _____
: _____
: _____

TO-DO ... prioritize pleasure

1. _____
2. _____
3. _____
   _____
   _____
   _____

BODY & WELLNESS My body helps me ...

DEVOTION My meditation will be ...

NOT WORKING ... don't hold back

STOP DOING ... clarity is power

GRATEFUL ... note WHY you're grateful

Because ...

SACRED

You will fail. Eventually. Whatever.

THURSDAY January 31, 2019

MY CORE DESIRED FEELINGS   *What I will do to feel the way I want to feel*

SCHEDULE ... work for Love

: _____
: _____
: _____
: _____
: _____
: _____
: _____
: _____
: _____
: _____
: _____
: _____
: _____
: _____
: _____
: _____

TO-DO ... do what lights you up

1. _____
2. _____
3. _____
   _____
   _____
   _____

BODY & WELLNESS My body is ...

DEVOTION I will dedicate this day to ...

NOT WORKING ... claim it. Tame it.

STOP DOING ... don't take any crap

GRATEFUL ... be a beacon of optimism   *Because ...*

If you look with your Soul, you will keep finding Light everywhere.

ELEGANT

THE PAST MONTH: Reflect. Clarify. Create.

ALWAYS BE CLARIFYING.
Knowing how you actually want to feel is the most potent form of clarity that you can have. Generating those feelings is the most powerfully creative thing you can do with your life.

MY CORE DESIRED FEELINGS
My CDFs are strongest in… I feel most aligned with… I'm moving toward…
I want to give more attention to…

MY GOALS & INTENTIONS
My goals are bringing my CDFs to life… I need to change up, refine or deepen…
To move closer to my goals & intentions I…

WHAT'S REALLY WORKING, YA!
I really felt [your CDF] when… This month I was so brilliant…
I created… I felt… I allowed… I accomplished…

WHAT NEEDS TO SHIFT
I felt disappointed… The challenge…

THE NEW MONTH: Envision. Intend. Energize.

GO WHERE YOU HAVEN'T GONE BEFORE.

"If you see your path laid out in front of you—Step one, Step two, Step three—you only know one thing...it is not your path. Your path is created in the moment of action. If you can see it laid out in front of you, you can be sure it is someone else's path. That is why you see it so clearly."
— Joseph Campbell

HOW I WILL

be stronger… softer… more determined… less uptight… more flexible… less constricted… more open… less accommodating… more accommodating… less worried… more generous… less doubtful… more trusting… less punishing… more pleasure-creating… less fearful… more loving…

TO MOVE TOWARD MY GOALS & INTENTIONS…

FEBRUARY
2019

FEBRUARY

Shima, shima, shima

Pronounced she-ma, this is a Hopi word for Love. Hold your hand on your heart and repeat until you feel the melting and expansion—108 times ideally. But start where you can.

	MONDAY	TUESDAY	WEDNESDAY
WEEK 5			
WEEK 6	**Mauni Amavasya (Hindu)** 4 ● New Moon in Aquarius	**Chinese New Year** 5	6
WEEK 7	11	12	13
WEEK 8	**President's Day (US)** 18 Sun enters Pisces	**Maghi Purnima (Hindu)** 19 ○ Full Moon in Virgo	20
WEEK 9	25	26	27

FEBRUARY

THURSDAY	FRIDAY	SATURDAY	SUNDAY
	Imbolc (Pagan) 1	**Groundhog Day** 2	Venus enters Capricorn 3
7	8	9	**Basant Panchami (Hindu)** 10 Mercury enters Pisces
Valentine's Day 14 Mars enters Taurus	15	16	17
21	22	23	24
28			

FRIDAY February 1, 2019 | *Imbolc (Pagan)*

MY CORE DESIRED FEELINGS

What I will do to feel the way I want to feel

SCHEDULE ... simplicity is freedom

: _____
: _____
: _____
: _____
: _____
: _____
: _____
: _____
: _____
: _____
: _____
: _____
: _____
: _____
: _____
: _____

TO-DO ... believe in yourself

1. _____
2. _____
3. _____
   _____
   _____
   _____

BODY & WELLNESS My body is telling me ...

DEVOTION I will light a candle for ...

NOT WORKING ... feel free

STOP DOING ... freedom is your birthright

GRATEFUL ... specificity intensifies gratitude

Because ...

INFINITE

Receive the Love that is being offered.

SATURDAY February 2, 2019
Groundhog Day

MY CORE DESIRED FEELINGS

TO-DO ... relax ... rebel ... rest

1. _____
2. _____
3. _____

_____
_____
_____

REFLECT
Hands on your heart, eyes closed, recite your CDFs and see what images arise.

SUNDAY February 3, 2019
Venus enters Capricorn

What I will do to feel the way I want to feel

TO-DO ... visualize your ideal life

1. _____
2. _____
3. _____

_____
_____
_____

ENVISION
What Core Desired Feeling(s) need extra attention this week?

SOUL PROMPT The easiest thing to do is

Look your desire in the eye.

INTEGRITY

MONDAY February 4, 2019 | *Mauni Amavasya (Hindu)* | ● *New Moon in Aquarius*

MY CORE DESIRED FEELINGS *What I will do to feel the way I want to feel*

SCHEDULE ... does it light you up?

: _____
: _____
: _____
: _____
: _____
: _____
: _____
: _____
: _____
: _____
: _____
: _____
: _____
: _____
: _____

TO-DO ... clarity creates simplicity

1. _____
2. _____
3. _____
_____
_____
_____

BODY & WELLNESS I will respect my body ...

DEVOTION I will have faith that ...

NOT WORKING ... does it feel light or heavy?

STOP DOING ... speak up

GRATEFUL ... ask for more   *Because ...*

ABUNDANCE

We are big spirits with human shortcomings.

TUESDAY February 5, 2019 | *Chinese New Year*

MY CORE DESIRED FEELINGS *What I will do to feel the way I want to feel*

SCHEDULE ... joy expands time

TO-DO ... keep your soul on the agenda

1. _____
2. _____
3. _____

BODY & WELLNESS My body knows ...

DEVOTION Devotion creates miracles.

NOT WORKING ... name it so you can change it

STOP DOING ... *No* makes way for *Yes*

GRATEFUL ... gratitude puts everything into perspective *Because ...*

Wide open space = deeper creativity.

BALANCED

WEDNESDAY February 6, 2019

MY CORE DESIRED FEELINGS

What I will do to feel the way I want to feel

SCHEDULE ... take up space

: _____
: _____
: _____
: _____
: _____
: _____
: _____
: _____
: _____
: _____
: _____
: _____
: _____
: _____
: _____

TO-DO ... make choices that liberate you

1. _____
2. _____
3. _____
   _____
   _____
   _____

BODY & WELLNESS I will tend to my body ...

DEVOTION I will contemplate ...

NOT WORKING ... don't hold back

STOP DOING ... clarity is power

GRATEFUL ... note WHY you're grateful

Because ...

ON FIRE

Let Love take over.

THURSDAY February 7, 2019

MY CORE DESIRED FEELINGS   *What I will do to feel the way I want to feel*

SCHEDULE ... what do you really want to happen?   **TO-DO** ... imagine

: _____   1. _____
: _____   2. _____
: _____   3. _____
: _____   _____
: _____   _____
: _____   _____
: _____
: _____   **BODY & WELLNESS** I will nourish my body ...
: _____
: _____
: _____   **DEVOTION** I will pray for (who/what) ...
: _____
: _____
: _____   **NOT WORKING** ... claim it. Tame it.
: _____
: _____
: _____   **STOP DOING** ... don't take any crap
: _____
: _____

GRATEFUL ... be a beacon of optimism   *Because ...*

Have the courage to enjoy it.   BOLD

FRIDAY February 8, 2019

MY CORE DESIRED FEELINGS

What I will do to feel the way I want to feel

SCHEDULE ... leave room for magic

: _____
: _____
: _____
: _____
: _____
: _____
: _____
: _____
: _____
: _____
: _____
: _____
: _____
: _____
: _____
: _____

TO-DO ... prioritize pleasure

1. _____
2. _____
3. _____
   _____
   _____
   _____

BODY & WELLNESS My body helps me ...

DEVOTION My meditation will be ...

NOT WORKING ... feel free

STOP DOING ... freedom is your birthright

GRATEFUL ... specificity intensifies gratitude

Because ...

LION-HEARTED

Consider the value of what you create for others.

SATURDAY February 9, 2019

MY CORE DESIRED FEELINGS

SUNDAY February 10, 2019
Basant Panchami (Hindu) | Mercury enters Pisces

What I will do to feel the way I want to feel

TO-DO ... let it be easy

1. _____
2. _____
3. _____
_____
_____
_____

REFLECT
The Core Desired Feeling closest to my heart is...

TO-DO ... make space for the light to enter

1. _____
2. _____
3. _____
_____
_____
_____

ENVISION
How are your Core Desired Feelings experienced in your body?

SOUL PROMPT I feel anxious when

Let your joy rise to the surface.

EMBODIED

MONDAY February 11, 2019

MY CORE DESIRED FEELINGS

What I will do to feel the way I want to feel

SCHEDULE ... work for Love

: _____
: _____
: _____
: _____
: _____
: _____
: _____
: _____
: _____
: _____
: _____
: _____
: _____
: _____
: _____
: _____

TO-DO ... do what lights you up

1. _____
2. _____
3. _____
   _____
   _____

BODY & WELLNESS My body is ...

DEVOTION I will dedicate this day to ...

NOT WORKING ... does it feel light or heavy?

STOP DOING ... speak up

GRATEFUL ... ask for more

Because ...

RAPTUROUS

You're in charge of your own karma.

TUESDAY February 12, 2019

MY CORE DESIRED FEELINGS

What I will do to feel the way I want to feel

SCHEDULE ... simplicity is freedom

: _____
: _____
: _____
: _____
: _____
: _____
: _____
: _____
: _____
: _____
: _____
: _____
: _____
: _____
: _____
: _____

TO-DO ... believe in yourself

1. _____
2. _____
3. _____
   _____
   _____
   _____

BODY & WELLNESS My body is telling me ...

DEVOTION I will light a candle for ...

NOT WORKING ... name it so you can change it

STOP DOING ... *No* makes way for *Yes*

GRATEFUL ... gratitude puts everything into perspective

Because ...

MAGNETIC

If you can't deliver your Truth with Love, then you should question why you're delivering it.

WEDNESDAY February 13, 2019

MY CORE DESIRED FEELINGS

What I will do to feel the way I want to feel

SCHEDULE ... does it light you up?

: _____
: _____
: _____
: _____
: _____
: _____
: _____
: _____
: _____
: _____
: _____
: _____
: _____
: _____
: _____
: _____

TO-DO ... clarity creates simplicity

1. _____
2. _____
3. _____
   _____
   _____
   _____

BODY & WELLNESS I will respect my body ...

DEVOTION I will have faith that ...

NOT WORKING ... don't hold back

STOP DOING ... clarity is power

GRATEFUL ... note WHY you're grateful

Because ...

POTENT

Your heart is a light source.

THURSDAY February 14, 2019 | *Valentine's Day | Mars enters Taurus*

MY CORE DESIRED FEELINGS   *What I will do to feel the way I want to feel*

SCHEDULE ... joy expands time

: _____
: _____
: _____
: _____
: _____
: _____
: _____
: _____
: _____
: _____
: _____
: _____
: _____
: _____
: _____
: _____

TO-DO ... keep your soul on the agenda

1. _____
2. _____
3. _____
   _____
   _____
   _____

BODY & WELLNESS My body knows ...

DEVOTION Devotion creates miracles.

NOT WORKING ... claim it. Tame it.

STOP DOING ... don't take any crap

GRATEFUL ... be a beacon of optimism   *Because ...*

Honor what's primal.

HEROIC

FRIDAY February 15, 2019

MY CORE DESIRED FEELINGS

What I will do to feel the way I want to feel

SCHEDULE ... take up space

: _____
: _____
: _____
: _____
: _____
: _____
: _____
: _____
: _____
: _____
: _____
: _____
: _____
: _____
: _____
: _____

TO-DO ... make choices that liberate you

1. _____
2. _____
3. _____
_____
_____
_____

BODY & WELLNESS I will tend to my body ...

DEVOTION I will contemplate ...

NOT WORKING ... feel free

STOP DOING ... freedom is your birthright

GRATEFUL ... specificity intensifies gratitude

Because ...

THRIVING

Take less shit. Way less.

SATURDAY February 16, 2019

MY CORE DESIRED FEELINGS

SUNDAY February 17, 2019

What I will do to feel the way I want to feel

TO-DO ... what would be comforting?

1. _____
2. _____
3. _____
_____
_____
_____

TO-DO ... relax ... rebel ... rest

1. _____
2. _____
3. _____
_____
_____
_____

REFLECT
A prayer: Thank you for the clarity and courage to make choices that favor my Core Desired Feelings.

ENVISION
A prayer: Thank you for guiding me to express and experience my Core Desired Feelings.

SOUL PROMPT What's different about me is that

Get your needs met.

MONDAY February 18, 2019 | *President's Day (US) | Sun enters Pisces*

MY CORE DESIRED FEELINGS   *What I will do to feel the way I want to feel*

SCHEDULE ... what do you really want to happen?   **TO-DO** ... imagine

: _____   1. _____
: _____   2. _____
: _____   3. _____
: _____   _____
: _____   _____
: _____   _____
: _____   **BODY & WELLNESS** I will nourish my body ...
: _____
: _____   **DEVOTION** I will pray for (who/what) ...
: _____
: _____   **NOT WORKING** ... does it feel light or heavy?
: _____
: _____   **STOP DOING** ... speak up
: _____
: _____

GRATEFUL ... ask for more   *Because ...*

ENGAGED

Joy is an indicator of deep wellness.

TUESDAY February 19, 2019 | *Maghi Purnima (Hindu) | ○ Full Moon in Virgo*

MY CORE DESIRED FEELINGS   *What I will do to feel the way I want to feel*

SCHEDULE ... leave room for magic

: _____
: _____
: _____
: _____
: _____
: _____
: _____
: _____
: _____
: _____
: _____
: _____
: _____
: _____
: _____
: _____
: _____

TO-DO ... prioritize pleasure

1. _____
2. _____
3. _____
   _____
   _____
   _____

BODY & WELLNESS My body helps me ...

DEVOTION My meditation will be ...

NOT WORKING ... name it so you can change it

STOP DOING ... *No* makes way for *Yes*

GRATEFUL ... gratitude puts everything into perspective   *Because ...*

But do you feel free?

RESONANCE

WEDNESDAY February 20, 2019

MY CORE DESIRED FEELINGS

What I will do to feel the way I want to feel

SCHEDULE ... work for Love

: _____
: _____
: _____
: _____
: _____
: _____
: _____
: _____
: _____
: _____
: _____
: _____
: _____
: _____
: _____
: _____

TO-DO ... do what lights you up

1. _____
2. _____
3. _____
_____
_____

BODY & WELLNESS My body is ...

DEVOTION I will dedicate this day to ...

NOT WORKING ... don't hold back

STOP DOING ... clarity is power

GRATEFUL ... note WHY you're grateful

Because ...

ROOTED

A woman without her own opinions is a tragedy.

THURSDAY February 21, 2019

MY CORE DESIRED FEELINGS

What I will do to feel the way I want to feel

SCHEDULE ... simplicity is freedom

: _____
: _____
: _____
: _____
: _____
: _____
: _____
: _____
: _____
: _____
: _____
: _____
: _____
: _____
: _____
: _____
: _____

TO-DO ... believe in yourself

1. _____
2. _____
3. _____
_____
_____
_____

BODY & WELLNESS My body is telling me ...

DEVOTION I will light a candle for ...

NOT WORKING ... claim it. Tame it.

STOP DOING ... don't take any crap

GRATEFUL ... be a beacon of optimism

Because ...

MAGNIFICENT

Time is NOT money.

FRIDAY February 22, 2019

MY CORE DESIRED FEELINGS

What I will do to feel the way I want to feel

SCHEDULE ... does it light you up?

: _____
: _____
: _____
: _____
: _____
: _____
: _____
: _____
: _____
: _____
: _____
: _____
: _____
: _____
: _____
: _____

TO-DO ... clarity creates simplicity

1. _____
2. _____
3. _____
   _____
   _____

BODY & WELLNESS I will respect my body ...

DEVOTION I will have faith that ...

NOT WORKING ... feel free

STOP DOING ... freedom is your birthright

GRATEFUL ... specificity intensifies gratitude

Because ...

PEACEFUL

Keep your longing for The Real Thing alive.

SATURDAY February 23, 2019

MY CORE DESIRED FEELINGS

TO-DO ... visualize your ideal life

1. _____
2. _____
3. _____
   _____
   _____
   _____

REFLECT
What Core Desired Feeling felt most alive in your life? Why/how?

SUNDAY February 24, 2019

What I will do to feel the way I want to feel

TO-DO ... let it be easy

1. _____
2. _____
3. _____
   _____
   _____
   _____

ENVISION
What rituals support your Core Desired Feelings?

SOUL PROMPT I bless

be proud of what you love

SHAKTI

MONDAY February 25, 2019

MY CORE DESIRED FEELINGS

What I will do to feel the way I want to feel

SCHEDULE ... joy expands time

: _____
: _____
: _____
: _____
: _____
: _____
: _____
: _____
: _____
: _____
: _____
: _____
: _____
: _____
: _____

TO-DO ... keep your soul on the agenda

1. _____
2. _____
3. _____
   _____
   _____
   _____

BODY & WELLNESS My body knows ...

DEVOTION Devotion creates miracles.

NOT WORKING ... does it feel light or heavy?

STOP DOING ... speak up

GRATEFUL ... ask for more

Because ...

ESSENTIAL

Kindness is a superpower.

TUESDAY February 26, 2019

MY CORE DESIRED FEELINGS

What I will do to feel the way I want to feel

SCHEDULE ... take up space

: _____
: _____
: _____
: _____
: _____
: _____
: _____
: _____
: _____
: _____
: _____
: _____
: _____
: _____
: _____
: _____

TO-DO ... make choices that liberate you

1. _____
2. _____
3. _____
_____
_____
_____

BODY & WELLNESS I will tend to my body ...

DEVOTION I will contemplate ...

NOT WORKING ... name it so you can change it

STOP DOING ... *No* makes way for *Yes*

GRATEFUL ... gratitude puts everything into perspective   *Because ...*

Are you willing to change?

VISIONARY

WEDNESDAY February 27, 2019

MY CORE DESIRED FEELINGS

What I will do to feel the way I want to feel

SCHEDULE ... what do you really want to happen?

: _____
: _____
: _____
: _____
: _____
: _____
: _____
: _____
: _____
: _____
: _____
: _____
: _____
: _____
: _____
: _____

TO-DO ... imagine

1. _____
2. _____
3. _____
   _____
   _____
   _____

BODY & WELLNESS I will nourish my body ...

DEVOTION I will pray for (who/what) ...

NOT WORKING ... don't hold back

STOP DOING ... clarity is power

GRATEFUL ... note WHY you're grateful

Because ...

HEALED

Sometimes, the most enlightened thing to do is FIGHT BACK.

THURSDAY February 28, 2019

MY CORE DESIRED FEELINGS   *What I will do to feel the way I want to feel*

SCHEDULE ... leave room for magic

: _____
: _____
: _____
: _____
: _____
: _____
: _____
: _____
: _____
: _____
: _____
: _____
: _____
: _____
: _____

TO-DO ... prioritize pleasure

1. _____
2. _____
3. _____
   _____
   _____
   _____

BODY & WELLNESS My body helps me ...

DEVOTION My meditation will be ...

NOT WORKING ... claim it. Tame it.

STOP DOING ... don't take any crap

GRATEFUL ... be a beacon of optimism   *Because ...*

Try staying open when you want to shut down, it changes everything.

DIVINE

THE PAST MONTH: Reflect. Clarify. Create.

KNOW YOUR WHY.

You're not chasing the goal itself—you're chasing the feelings that you hope attaining those goals will give you.

MY CORE DESIRED FEELINGS

My CDFs are strongest in… I feel most aligned with… I'm moving toward…
I want to give more attention to…

MY GOALS & INTENTIONS

My goals are bringing my CDFs to life… I need to change up, refine or deepen…
To move closer to my goals & intentions I…

WHAT'S REALLY WORKING, YA!

I really felt [your CDF] when… This month I was so brilliant…
I created… I felt… I allowed… I accomplished…

WHAT NEEDS TO SHIFT

I felt disappointed… The challenge…

THE NEW MONTH: Envision. Intend. Energize.

STRIKE THE WORD OBLIGATION FROM YOUR VOCABULARY.

"Freedom...is not being rid of responsibilities; it is being free of random shoulds and oughts. Freedom doesn't dwell in randomness but in conscious choice."
— Gertrud Mueller Nelson

HOW I WILL

be stronger… softer… more determined… less uptight… more flexible… less constricted… more open… less accommodating… more accommodating… less worried… more generous… less doubtful… more trusting… less punishing… more pleasure-creating… less fearful… more loving…

TO MOVE TOWARD MY GOALS & INTENTIONS…

MARCH
2019

Sacred.
Expansive.
Nurturing.
All-inclusive.
Glowing.
Wisdom.
Ever-present.
Self-sustaining.
All-knowing.

These are the words of power from the Creation Space Meditation. Silently, out loud, or as a chant, say each word with your most Sacred Intention, your whole heart, feeling each word deeply, on a cellular level.

MARCH

MONDAY	TUESDAY	WEDNESDAY
WEEK 9		
Labour Day (AUS) **Maha Shivaratri (Hindu)** 4	Mercury stations Retrograde in Pisces 5	● New Moon in Pisces Uranus enters Taurus 6
WEEK 10		
Commonwealth Day (CAN) 11	12	13
WEEK 11		
18	19	**Spring Equinox/ Ostara (Pagan)** 20 ○ Full Moon in Libra Sun enters Aries
WEEK 12		
25	Venus enters Pisces 26	27
WEEK 13		

MARCH

THURSDAY	FRIDAY	SATURDAY	SUNDAY
	1 Venus enters Aquarius	2	3
7	8 International Women's Day	9	10 Daylight Saving Time starts (CAN, US)
14	15	16	17 St. Patrick's Day
21 **Holi (Hindu) Purim (Jewish holiday)**	22	23	24
28 Mercury stations Direct in Pisces	29	30 Mars enters Gemini	31

FRIDAY March 1, 2019 | *Venus enters Aquarius*

MY CORE DESIRED FEELINGS

What I will do to feel the way I want to feel

SCHEDULE ... work for Love

: _____
: _____
: _____
: _____
: _____
: _____
: _____
: _____
: _____
: _____
: _____
: _____
: _____
: _____
: _____

TO-DO ... do what lights you up

1. _____
2. _____
3. _____
_____
_____

BODY & WELLNESS My body is ...

DEVOTION I will dedicate this day to ...

NOT WORKING ... feel free

STOP DOING ... freedom is your birthright

GRATEFUL ... specificity intensifies gratitude

Because ...

EFFORTLESS

Shift the focus from "being loving" to "being Love itself".

SATURDAY March 2, 2019

MY CORE DESIRED FEELINGS

TO-DO ... make space for the light to enter

1. _____
2. _____
3. _____
_____
_____
_____

REFLECT
Which Core Desired Feeling seems farthest away? How do you feel about that?

SOUL PROMPT If only I could

SUNDAY March 3, 2019

What I will do to feel the way I want to feel

TO-DO ... what would be comforting?

1. _____
2. _____
3. _____
_____
_____
_____

ENVISION
What would help you feel your Core Desired Feelings this week?

You can't really know your power until you exercise it.

WILD

MONDAY March 4, 2019 | *Labour Day (AUS) | Maha Shivaratri (Hindu)*

MY CORE DESIRED FEELINGS   *What I will do to feel the way I want to feel*

SCHEDULE ... simplicity is freedom

: _____
: _____
: _____
: _____
: _____
: _____
: _____
: _____
: _____
: _____
: _____
: _____
: _____
: _____
: _____
: _____

TO-DO ... believe in yourself

1. _____
2. _____
3. _____
   _____
   _____
   _____

BODY & WELLNESS My body is telling me ...

DEVOTION I will light a candle for ...

NOT WORKING ... does it feel light or heavy?

STOP DOING ... speak up

GRATEFUL ... ask for more   *Because ...*

SENSUOUS

Seriously, it does NOT MATTER what they think.

TUESDAY March 5, 2019 | *Mercury stations Retrograde in Pisces*

MY CORE DESIRED FEELINGS   *What I will do to feel the way I want to feel*

SCHEDULE ... does it light you up?

  : _____
  : _____
  : _____
  : _____
  : _____
  : _____
  : _____
  : _____
  : _____
  : _____
  : _____
  : _____
  : _____
  : _____
  : _____
  : _____

TO-DO ... clarity creates simplicity

1. _____
2. _____
3. _____
   _____
   _____
   _____

BODY & WELLNESS I will respect my body ...

DEVOTION I will have faith that ...

NOT WORKING ... name it so you can change it

STOP DOING ... *No* makes way for *Yes*

GRATEFUL ... gratitude puts everything into perspective   *Because ...*

You are the temple.

TRIBAL

WEDNESDAY March 6, 2019 | ● New Moon in Pisces | Uranus enters Taurus

MY CORE DESIRED FEELINGS   *What I will do to feel the way I want to feel*

SCHEDULE ... joy expands time   **TO-DO** ... keep your soul on the agenda

: _____   1. _____
: _____   2. _____
: _____   3. _____
: _____   _____
: _____   _____
: _____   _____
: _____   **BODY & WELLNESS** My body knows ...
: _____
: _____   **DEVOTION** Devotion creates miracles.
: _____
: _____
: _____   **NOT WORKING** ... don't hold back
: _____
: _____
: _____   **STOP DOING** ... clarity is power
: _____
: _____

GRATEFUL ... note WHY you're grateful   *Because ...*

ENLIGHTENING

It's about ongoing practice, not permanence.

THURSDAY March 7, 2019

MY CORE DESIRED FEELINGS

What I will do to feel the way I want to feel

SCHEDULE ... take up space

: _____
: _____
: _____
: _____
: _____
: _____
: _____
: _____
: _____
: _____
: _____
: _____
: _____
: _____
: _____
: _____
: _____

TO-DO ... make choices that liberate you

1. _____
2. _____
3. _____
_____
_____
_____

BODY & WELLNESS I will tend to my body ...

DEVOTION I will contemplate ...

NOT WORKING ... claim it. Tame it.

STOP DOING ... don't take any crap

GRATEFUL ... be a beacon of optimism

Because ...

Safety is only a habit.

COZY

FRIDAY March 8, 2019 | *International Women's Day*

MY CORE DESIRED FEELINGS   *What I will do to feel the way I want to feel*

SCHEDULE ... what do you really want to happen?   **TO-DO** ... imagine

: _____   1. _____
: _____   2. _____
: _____   3. _____
: _____   _____
: _____   _____
: _____   _____
: _____
: _____   **BODY & WELLNESS** I will nourish my body ...
: _____
: _____   **DEVOTION** I will pray for (who/what) ...
: _____
: _____   **NOT WORKING** ... feel free
: _____
: _____
: _____   **STOP DOING** ... freedom is your birthright
: _____
: _____

GRATEFUL ... specificity intensifies gratitude   *Because ...*

FLUID

Don't privilege overly needy types.

SATURDAY March 9, 2019

MY CORE DESIRED FEELINGS

TO-DO ... relax ... rebel ... rest

1. _____
2. _____
3. _____
   _____
   _____
   _____

REFLECT
When you are feeling your CDFs, how does that help you be of more service to others?

SOUL PROMPT I'm overflowing with

SUNDAY March 10, 2019
Daylight Saving Time starts (CAN, US)

What I will do to feel the way I want to feel

TO-DO ... visualize your ideal life

1. _____
2. _____
3. _____
   _____
   _____
   _____

ENVISION
How will you show up in the world as one of your CDFs?

When you trust that your pain is/was real, you'll trust your joy more.

CENTERED

MONDAY March 11, 2019 | *Commonwealth Day (CAN)*

MY CORE DESIRED FEELINGS   *What I will do to feel the way I want to feel*

SCHEDULE ... leave room for magic   **TO-DO** ... prioritize pleasure

: _____   1. _____
: _____   2. _____
: _____   3. _____
: _____   _____
: _____   _____
: _____   _____
: _____   **BODY & WELLNESS** My body helps me ...
: _____
: _____
: _____   **DEVOTION** My meditation will be ...
: _____
: _____
: _____   **NOT WORKING** ... does it feel light or heavy?
: _____
: _____
: _____   **STOP DOING** ... speak up
: _____
: _____

GRATEFUL ... ask for more   *Because ...*

GROUNDED

If you want the best out of life, it requires the best of you.

TUESDAY March 12, 2019

MY CORE DESIRED FEELINGS   *What I will do to feel the way I want to feel*

SCHEDULE ... work for Love

: _____
: _____
: _____
: _____
: _____
: _____
: _____
: _____
: _____
: _____
: _____
: _____
: _____
: _____
: _____

TO-DO ... do what lights you up

1. _____
2. _____
3. _____
   _____
   _____
   _____

BODY & WELLNESS My body is ...

DEVOTION I will dedicate this day to ...

NOT WORKING ... name it so you can change it

STOP DOING ... *No* makes way for *Yes*

GRATEFUL ... gratitude puts everything into perspective   *Because ...*

FREE-FLOWING

Procrastination can be a form of intuition.

WEDNESDAY March 13, 2019

MY CORE DESIRED FEELINGS

What I will do to feel the way I want to feel

SCHEDULE ... simplicity is freedom

: _____
: _____
: _____
: _____
: _____
: _____
: _____
: _____
: _____
: _____
: _____
: _____
: _____
: _____
: _____

TO-DO ... believe in yourself

1. _____
2. _____
3. _____
   _____
   _____

BODY & WELLNESS My body is telling me ...

DEVOTION I will light a candle for ...

NOT WORKING ... don't hold back

STOP DOING ... clarity is power

GRATEFUL ... note WHY you're grateful

Because ...

TETHERED

Love without doubt.

THURSDAY March 14, 2019

MY CORE DESIRED FEELINGS   *What I will do to feel the way I want to feel*

SCHEDULE ... does it light you up?

: _____
: _____
: _____
: _____
: _____
: _____
: _____
: _____
: _____
: _____
: _____
: _____
: _____
: _____
: _____
: _____
: _____

TO-DO ... clarity creates simplicity

1. _____
2. _____
3. _____
   _____
   _____
   _____

BODY & WELLNESS I will respect my body ...

DEVOTION I will have faith that ...

NOT WORKING ... claim it. Tame it.

STOP DOING ... don't take any crap

GRATEFUL ... be a beacon of optimism   *Because ...*

Notice when your dream has come true.

WHOLESOME

FRIDAY March 15, 2019

MY CORE DESIRED FEELINGS

What I will do to feel the way I want to feel

SCHEDULE ... joy expands time

: _____
: _____
: _____
: _____
: _____
: _____
: _____
: _____
: _____
: _____
: _____
: _____
: _____
: _____
: _____
: _____

TO-DO ... keep your soul on the agenda

1. _____
2. _____
3. _____
   _____
   _____

BODY & WELLNESS My body knows ...

DEVOTION Devotion creates miracles.

NOT WORKING ... feel free

STOP DOING ... freedom is your birthright

GRATEFUL ... specificity intensifies gratitude

Because ...

INTIMATE

Truth distortion is part of Truth clarification.

SATURDAY March 16, 2019

MY CORE DESIRED FEELINGS

татор... let it be easy

1. _____
2. _____
3. _____

REFLECT
Have a conversation with one of your CDFs, ask it to give you some guidance.

SUNDAY March 17, 2019
St. Patrick's Day

What I will do to feel the way I want to feel

TO-DO... make space for the light to enter

1. _____
2. _____
3. _____

ENVISION
What spaces or places embody your Core Desired Feelings?

SOUL PROMPT I don't regret

Freedom is where love flows endlessly.

BOUNDLESS

MONDAY March 18, 2019

MY CORE DESIRED FEELINGS

What I will do to feel the way I want to feel

SCHEDULE ... take up space

: _____
: _____
: _____
: _____
: _____
: _____
: _____
: _____
: _____
: _____
: _____
: _____
: _____
: _____
: _____
: _____

TO-DO ... make choices that liberate you

1. _____
2. _____
3. _____
   _____
   _____
   _____

BODY & WELLNESS I will tend to my body ...

DEVOTION I will contemplate ...

NOT WORKING ... does it feel light or heavy?

STOP DOING ... speak up

GRATEFUL ... ask for more

Because ...

FLOURISHING

you are free to choose

TUESDAY March 19, 2019

MY CORE DESIRED FEELINGS

What I will do to feel the way I want to feel

SCHEDULE ... what do you really want to happen?

: _____
: _____
: _____
: _____
: _____
: _____
: _____
: _____
: _____
: _____
: _____
: _____
: _____
: _____
: _____
: _____
: _____
: _____

TO-DO ... imagine

1. _____
2. _____
3. _____
_____
_____
_____

BODY & WELLNESS I will nourish my body ...

DEVOTION I will pray for (who/what) ...

NOT WORKING ... name it so you can change it

STOP DOING ... *No* makes way for *Yes*

GRATEFUL ... gratitude puts everything into perspective

Because ...

Thank the lies for showing you the Truth.

LOVE

WEDNESDAY March 20, 2019 | *Spring Equinox/Ostara (Pagan)* | O *Full Moon in Libra* | Sun enters Aries

MY CORE DESIRED FEELINGS

What I will do to feel the way I want to feel

SCHEDULE ... leave room for magic

: _____
: _____
: _____
: _____
: _____
: _____
: _____
: _____
: _____
: _____
: _____
: _____
: _____
: _____
: _____
: _____

TO-DO ... prioritize pleasure

1. _____
2. _____
3. _____
   _____
   _____
   _____

BODY & WELLNESS My body helps me ...

DEVOTION My meditation will be ...

NOT WORKING ... don't hold back

STOP DOING ... clarity is power

GRATEFUL ... note WHY you're grateful

Because ...

DEPTH

Stand where you feel strong.

THURSDAY March 21, 2019 | *Holi (Hindu) | Purim (Jewish holiday)*

MY CORE DESIRED FEELINGS   *What I will do to feel the way I want to feel*

SCHEDULE ... work for Love

: _____
: _____
: _____
: _____
: _____
: _____
: _____
: _____
: _____
: _____
: _____
: _____
: _____
: _____
: _____
: _____

TO-DO ... do what lights you up

1. _____
2. _____
3. _____
   _____
   _____
   _____

BODY & WELLNESS My body is ...

DEVOTION I will dedicate this day to ...

NOT WORKING ... claim it. Tame it.

STOP DOING ... don't take any crap

GRATEFUL ... be a beacon of optimism   *Because ...*

CREATIVE

Speak up. Speak out. Speak to be. Speak to make. Speak to heal.

FRIDAY March 22, 2019

MY CORE DESIRED FEELINGS

What I will do to feel the way I want to feel

SCHEDULE ... simplicity is freedom

: _____
: _____
: _____
: _____
: _____
: _____
: _____
: _____
: _____
: _____
: _____
: _____
: _____
: _____
: _____

TO-DO ... believe in yourself

1. _____
2. _____
3. _____
   _____
   _____
   _____

BODY & WELLNESS My body is telling me ...

DEVOTION I will light a candle for ...

NOT WORKING ... feel free

STOP DOING ... freedom is your birthright

GRATEFUL ... specificity intensifies gratitude

Because ...

CHOSEN

Have an opinion. Use it.

SATURDAY March 23, 2019

MY CORE DESIRED FEELINGS

SUNDAY March 24, 2019

What I will do to feel the way I want to feel

TO-DO ... what would be comforting?

1. _____
2. _____
3. _____
_____
_____
_____

TO-DO ... relax ... rebel ... rest

1. _____
2. _____
3. _____
_____
_____
_____

REFLECT
Hands on your heart, eyes closed, recite your CDFs and see what images arise.

ENVISION
What Core Desired Feeling(s) need extra attention this week?

SOUL PROMPT My energy is

You don't have to be grateful for all of it. Be grateful for what you learned from it.

SOFTNESS

MONDAY March 25, 2019

MY CORE DESIRED FEELINGS

What I will do to feel the way I want to feel

SCHEDULE ... does it light you up?

: _____
: _____
: _____
: _____
: _____
: _____
: _____
: _____
: _____
: _____
: _____
: _____
: _____
: _____
: _____
: _____
: _____

TO-DO ... clarity creates simplicity

1. _____
2. _____
3. _____
   _____
   _____
   _____

BODY & WELLNESS I will respect my body ...

DEVOTION I will have faith that ...

NOT WORKING ... does it feel light or heavy?

STOP DOING ... speak up

GRATEFUL ... ask for more

Because ...

KARMIC

Surprise your doubts with action.

TUESDAY March 26, 2019 | *Venus enters Pisces*

MY CORE DESIRED FEELINGS   *What I will do to feel the way I want to feel*

SCHEDULE ... joy expands time

TO-DO ... keep your soul on the agenda

1. _____
2. _____
3. _____

BODY & WELLNESS My body knows ...

DEVOTION Devotion creates miracles.

NOT WORKING ... name it so you can change it

STOP DOING ... *No* makes way for *Yes*

GRATEFUL ... gratitude puts everything into perspective   *Because ...*

The first thing to tell yourself when you're in hell: this pain WILL end.

UNLEASHED

WEDNESDAY March 27, 2019

MY CORE DESIRED FEELINGS

What I will do to feel the way I want to feel

SCHEDULE ... take up space

: _____
: _____
: _____
: _____
: _____
: _____
: _____
: _____
: _____
: _____
: _____
: _____
: _____
: _____
: _____
: _____

TO-DO ... make choices that liberate you

1. _____
2. _____
3. _____
   _____
   _____
   _____

BODY & WELLNESS I will tend to my body ...

DEVOTION I will contemplate ...

NOT WORKING ... don't hold back

STOP DOING ... clarity is power

GRATEFUL ... note WHY you're grateful

Because ...

SURRENDER

Truth is a magical power surge.

THURSDAY March 28, 2019 | *Mercury stations Direct in Pisces*

MY CORE DESIRED FEELINGS   *What I will do to feel the way I want to feel*

SCHEDULE ... what do you really want to happen?

: _____
: _____
: _____
: _____
: _____
: _____
: _____
: _____
: _____
: _____
: _____
: _____
: _____
: _____
: _____
: _____
: _____

TO-DO ... imagine

1. _____
2. _____
3. _____
_____
_____
_____

BODY & WELLNESS I will nourish my body ...

DEVOTION I will pray for (who/what) ...

NOT WORKING ... claim it. Tame it.

STOP DOING ... don't take any crap

GRATEFUL ... be a beacon of optimism   *Because ...*

Sanction it with your Love.

ENTHRALLED

FRIDAY March 29, 2019

MY CORE DESIRED FEELINGS

What I will do to feel the way I want to feel

SCHEDULE ... leave room for magic

: _____
: _____
: _____
: _____
: _____
: _____
: _____
: _____
: _____
: _____
: _____
: _____
: _____
: _____
: _____
: _____

TO-DO ... prioritize pleasure

1. _____
2. _____
3. _____
   _____
   _____
   _____

BODY & WELLNESS My body helps me ...

DEVOTION My meditation will be ...

NOT WORKING ... feel free

STOP DOING ... freedom is your birthright

GRATEFUL ... specificity intensifies gratitude

Because ...

SHINE

Notice all the prayers in your life that have been answered.

SATURDAY March 30, 2019
Mars enters Gemini

MY CORE DESIRED FEELINGS

TO-DO ... visualize your ideal life

1. _____
2. _____
3. _____
_____
_____
_____

REFLECT
The Core Desired Feeling closest to my heart is...

SUNDAY March 31, 2019

What I will do to feel the way I want to feel

TO-DO ... let it be easy

1. _____
2. _____
3. _____
_____
_____
_____

ENVISION
How are your Core Desired Feelings experienced in your body?

SOUL PROMPT I forgive

Grace is the cousin of synchronicity.

ECSTATIC

THE PAST MONTH: Reflect. Clarify. Create.

YOU KNOW.
Your feelings are road signs that point you to your Soul. The "worse" or more disconnected you feel, the further you are from your truth. The clearer, stronger, more joyful you feel, then the closer you are to your truth.

MY CORE DESIRED FEELINGS
My CDFs are strongest in… I feel most aligned with… I'm moving toward…
I want to give more attention to…

MY GOALS & INTENTIONS
My goals are bringing my CDFs to life… I need to change up, refine or deepen…
To move closer to my goals & intentions I…

WHAT'S REALLY WORKING, YA!
I really felt [your CDF] when… This month I was so brilliant…
I created… I felt… I allowed… I accomplished…

WHAT NEEDS TO SHIFT
I felt disappointed… The challenge…

THE NEW MONTH: Envision. Intend. Energize.

JUST BEGIN.
"The best time to plant a tree was 20 years ago.
The second best time is now."
— Chinese Proverb

HOW I WILL

be stronger… softer… more determined… less uptight… more flexible… less constricted… more open… less accommodating… more accommodating… less worried… more generous… less doubtful… more trusting… less punishing… more pleasure-creating… less fearful… more loving…

TO MOVE TOWARD MY GOALS & INTENTIONS…

APRIL
2019

The way is free of obstacles. The signs are clear. I move with powerful grace.

Imagine yourself arriving at your fulfilled desire.

MONDAY	TUESDAY	WEDNESDAY
1	2	**Lailat al Miraj (Islam)** 3
WEEK 14		
8	9	Jupiter stations Retrograde in Sagittarius 10
WEEK 15		
15	Mercury enters Aries 16	17
WEEK 16		
Earth Day 22	23	Pluto stations Retrograde in Capricorn 24
WEEK 17		
Saturn stations Retrograde in Capricorn 29	30	
WEEK 18		

THURSDAY	FRIDAY	SATURDAY	SUNDAY
4	5 ● New Moon in Aries	6	7 **Daylight Saving Time ends (AUS)**
11	12	13	14 **Palm Sunday (Christian)**
18	19 **Good Friday (Christian)** ○ Full Moon in Libra	20 **Passover begins (Jewish holiday)** Sun enters Taurus Venus enters Aries	21 **Laylat al-Bara'at (Islam)** **Easter Sunday (Christian)**
25 **ANZAC Day (AUS)**	26	27 **Passover ends - evening (Jewish holiday)**	28

APRIL

MONDAY April 1, 2019

MY CORE DESIRED FEELINGS *What I will do to feel the way I want to feel*

SCHEDULE ... work for Love

: _____
: _____
: _____
: _____
: _____
: _____
: _____
: _____
: _____
: _____
: _____
: _____
: _____
: _____
: _____
: _____

TO-DO ... do what lights you up

1. _____
2. _____
3. _____
   _____
   _____

BODY & WELLNESS My body is ...

DEVOTION I will dedicate this day to ...

NOT WORKING ... does it feel light or heavy?

STOP DOING ... speak up

GRATEFUL ... ask for more   *Because ...*

OPEN HEARTED

Do whatever it takes to make it better.

TUESDAY April 2, 2019

MY CORE DESIRED FEELINGS   *What I will do to feel the way I want to feel*

SCHEDULE ... simplicity is freedom

: _____
: _____
: _____
: _____
: _____
: _____
: _____
: _____
: _____
: _____
: _____
: _____
: _____
: _____
: _____
: _____

TO-DO ... believe in yourself

1. _____
2. _____
3. _____
   _____
   _____
   _____

BODY & WELLNESS My body is telling me ...

DEVOTION I will light a candle for ...

NOT WORKING ... name it so you can change it

STOP DOING ... *No* makes way for *Yes*

GRATEFUL ... gratitude puts everything into perspective   *Because ...*

Fearlessness is a fat myth.

ELEVATED

WEDNESDAY April 3, 2019 | *Lailat al Miraj (Islam)*

MY CORE DESIRED FEELINGS　　　　　　　　　　*What I will do to feel the way I want to feel*

SCHEDULE ... does it light you up?

: _____
: _____
: _____
: _____
: _____
: _____
: _____
: _____
: _____
: _____
: _____
: _____
: _____
: _____
: _____
: _____
: _____

TO-DO ... clarity creates simplicity

1. _____
2. _____
3. _____
   _____
   _____
   _____
   _____

BODY & WELLNESS I will respect my body ...

DEVOTION I will have faith that ...

NOT WORKING ... don't hold back

STOP DOING ... clarity is power

GRATEFUL ... note WHY you're grateful　　　　*Because ...*

INTUITIVE

You are changing.

THURSDAY April 4, 2019

MY CORE DESIRED FEELINGS *What I will do to feel the way I want to feel*

SCHEDULE ... joy expands time

: _____
: _____
: _____
: _____
: _____
: _____
: _____
: _____
: _____
: _____
: _____
: _____
: _____
: _____
: _____
: _____
: _____

TO-DO ... keep your soul on the agenda

1. _____
2. _____
3. _____
_____
_____
_____

BODY & WELLNESS My body knows ...

DEVOTION Devotion creates miracles.

NOT WORKING ... claim it. Tame it.

STOP DOING ... don't take any crap

GRATEFUL ... be a beacon of optimism   *Because ...*

You can't go wrong if you commit to being of service.

AWAKENED

FRIDAY April 5, 2019 | ● *New Moon in Aries*

MY CORE DESIRED FEELINGS

What I will do to feel the way I want to feel

SCHEDULE ... take up space

: _____
: _____
: _____
: _____
: _____
: _____
: _____
: _____
: _____
: _____
: _____
: _____
: _____
: _____
: _____
: _____

TO-DO ... make choices that liberate you

1. _____
2. _____
3. _____
   _____
   _____
   _____

BODY & WELLNESS I will tend to my body ...

DEVOTION I will contemplate ...

NOT WORKING ... feel free

STOP DOING ... freedom is your birthright

GRATEFUL ... specificity intensifies gratitude

Because ...

DEEPLY

It's all divine timing.

SATURDAY April 6, 2019

MY CORE DESIRED FEELINGS

TO-DO ... make space for the light to enter

1. _____
2. _____
3. _____
   _____
   _____
   _____

REFLECT
A prayer: Thank you for the clarity and courage to make choices that favor my Core Desired Feelings.

SUNDAY April 7, 2019
Daylight Saving Time ends (AUS)

What I will do to feel the way I want to feel

TO-DO ... what would be comforting?

1. _____
2. _____
3. _____
   _____
   _____
   _____

ENVISION
A prayer: Thank you for guiding me to express and experience my Core Desired Feelings.

SOUL PROMPT I will be

Spill blessings every every everywhere.

CONNECTED

MONDAY April 8, 2019

MY CORE DESIRED FEELINGS

What I will do to feel the way I want to feel

SCHEDULE ... what do you really want to happen?

: _____
: _____
: _____
: _____
: _____
: _____
: _____
: _____
: _____
: _____
: _____
: _____
: _____
: _____
: _____
: _____
: _____

TO-DO ... imagine

1. _____
2. _____
3. _____
   _____
   _____
   _____

BODY & WELLNESS I will nourish my body ...

DEVOTION I will pray for (who/what) ...

NOT WORKING ... does it feel light or heavy?

STOP DOING ... speak up

GRATEFUL ... ask for more

Because ...

DELIGHT

Embrace the intensity.

TUESDAY April 9, 2019

MY CORE DESIRED FEELINGS

What I will do to feel the way I want to feel

SCHEDULE ... leave room for magic

: _____
: _____
: _____
: _____
: _____
: _____
: _____
: _____
: _____
: _____
: _____
: _____
: _____
: _____
: _____
: _____
: _____

TO-DO ... prioritize pleasure

1. _____
2. _____
3. _____
   _____
   _____
   _____

BODY & WELLNESS My body helps me ...

DEVOTION My meditation will be ...

NOT WORKING ... name it so you can change it

STOP DOING ... *No* makes way for *Yes*

GRATEFUL ... gratitude puts everything into perspective

Because ...

FORGIVING

Your definition of what's sacred will change over time.

WEDNESDAY April 10, 2019 | *Jupiter stations Retrograde in Sagittarius*

MY CORE DESIRED FEELINGS   *What I will do to feel the way I want to feel*

SCHEDULE ... work for Love

: _____
: _____
: _____
: _____
: _____
: _____
: _____
: _____
: _____
: _____
: _____
: _____
: _____
: _____
: _____
: _____

TO-DO ... do what lights you up

1. _____
2. _____
3. _____
   _____
   _____

BODY & WELLNESS My body is ...

DEVOTION I will dedicate this day to ...

NOT WORKING ... don't hold back

STOP DOING ... clarity is power

GRATEFUL ... note WHY you're grateful   *Because ...*

REMARKABLE

You have multiple possible futures—each of which could be equally incredible.

THURSDAY April 11, 2019

MY CORE DESIRED FEELINGS — *What I will do to feel the way I want to feel*

SCHEDULE ... simplicity is freedom

: _____
: _____
: _____
: _____
: _____
: _____
: _____
: _____
: _____
: _____
: _____
: _____
: _____
: _____
: _____
: _____

TO-DO ... believe in yourself

1. _____
2. _____
3. _____
   _____
   _____
   _____

BODY & WELLNESS My body is telling me ...

DEVOTION I will light a candle for ...

NOT WORKING ... claim it. Tame it.

STOP DOING ... don't take any crap

GRATEFUL ... be a beacon of optimism   *Because ...*

Want to bring out the best in people? Ask them how they want to feel.

CHARMED

FRIDAY April 12, 2019

MY CORE DESIRED FEELINGS

What I will do to feel the way I want to feel

SCHEDULE ... does it light you up?

: _____
: _____
: _____
: _____
: _____
: _____
: _____
: _____
: _____
: _____
: _____
: _____
: _____
: _____
: _____
: _____
: _____

TO-DO ... clarity creates simplicity

1. _____
2. _____
3. _____
_____
_____
_____

BODY & WELLNESS I will respect my body ...

DEVOTION I will have faith that ...

NOT WORKING ... feel free

STOP DOING ... freedom is your birthright

GRATEFUL ... specificity intensifies gratitude

Because ...

PRACTICAL

Question if you still Love what you once Loved.

SATURDAY April 13, 2019

MY CORE DESIRED FEELINGS

TO-DO ... relax ... rebel ... rest

1. _____
2. _____
3. _____
   _____
   _____
   _____

REFLECT
What Core Desired Feeling felt most alive in your life? Why/how?

SUNDAY April 14, 2019
Palm Sunday (Christian)

What I will do to feel the way I want to feel

TO-DO ... visualize your ideal life

1. _____
2. _____
3. _____
   _____
   _____
   _____

ENVISION
What rituals support your Core Desired Feelings?

SOUL PROMPT My bedtime ritual

It helps to be clear on exactly what you're leaving behind.

SOLACE

MONDAY April 15, 2019

MY CORE DESIRED FEELINGS

What I will do to feel the way I want to feel

SCHEDULE ... joy expands time

: _____
: _____
: _____
: _____
: _____
: _____
: _____
: _____
: _____
: _____
: _____
: _____
: _____
: _____
: _____

TO-DO ... keep your soul on the agenda

1. _____
2. _____
3. _____
  _____
  _____
  _____

BODY & WELLNESS My body knows ...

DEVOTION Devotion creates miracles.

NOT WORKING ... does it feel light or heavy?

STOP DOING ... speak up

GRATEFUL ... ask for more

Because ...

UNTETHERED

Manifestation requires clear intention.

TUESDAY April 16, 2019 | *Mercury enters Aries*

MY CORE DESIRED FEELINGS   *What I will do to feel the way I want to feel*

SCHEDULE ... take up space

: _____
: _____
: _____
: _____
: _____
: _____
: _____
: _____
: _____
: _____
: _____
: _____
: _____
: _____
: _____
: _____

TO-DO ... make choices that liberate you

1. _____
2. _____
3. _____
_____
_____
_____

BODY & WELLNESS I will tend to my body ...

DEVOTION I will contemplate ...

NOT WORKING ... name it so you can change it

STOP DOING ... *No* makes way for *Yes*

GRATEFUL ... gratitude puts everything into perspective   *Because ...*

Forgive yourself for not wanting to forgive.

RESPLENDENT

WEDNESDAY April 17, 2019

MY CORE DESIRED FEELINGS

What I will do to feel the way I want to feel

SCHEDULE ... what do you really want to happen?

: _____
: _____
: _____
: _____
: _____
: _____
: _____
: _____
: _____
: _____
: _____
: _____
: _____
: _____
: _____
: _____
: _____

TO-DO ... imagine

1. _____
2. _____
3. _____
   _____
   _____
   _____

BODY & WELLNESS I will nourish my body ...

DEVOTION I will pray for (who/what) ...

NOT WORKING ... don't hold back

STOP DOING ... clarity is power

GRATEFUL ... note WHY you're grateful

Because ...

INSPIRA-TIONAL

Comparison is a killer.

THURSDAY April 18, 2019

MY CORE DESIRED FEELINGS   *What I will do to feel the way I want to feel*

SCHEDULE ... leave room for magic   **TO-DO** ... prioritize pleasure

: _____   1. _____
: _____   2. _____
: _____   3. _____
: _____   _____
: _____   _____
: _____   _____
: _____
: _____   **BODY & WELLNESS** My body helps me ...
: _____
: _____   **DEVOTION** My meditation will be ...
: _____
: _____
: _____   **NOT WORKING** ... claim it. Tame it.
: _____
: _____
: _____   **STOP DOING** ... don't take any crap
: _____
: _____

GRATEFUL ... be a beacon of optimism   *Because ...*

Create an ideal story of your future and tell it over and over again.

MOTIVA-
TIONAL

FRIDAY April 19, 2019 | *Good Friday (Christian)* | ○ *Full Moon in Libra*

MY CORE DESIRED FEELINGS

What I will do to feel the way I want to feel

SCHEDULE ... work for Love

: _____
: _____
: _____
: _____
: _____
: _____
: _____
: _____
: _____
: _____
: _____
: _____
: _____
: _____
: _____
: _____

TO-DO ... do what lights you up

1. _____
2. _____
3. _____
   _____
   _____

BODY & WELLNESS My body is ...

DEVOTION I will dedicate this day to ...

NOT WORKING ... feel free

STOP DOING ... freedom is your birthright

GRATEFUL ... specificity intensifies gratitude

Because ...

GRACIOUS

If knowledge is power, then curiosity is the muscle.

SATURDAY April 20, 2019

Passover begins (Jewish holiday) | Sun enters Taurus
Venus enters Aries

MY CORE DESIRED FEELINGS

TO-DO ... let it be easy

1. _____
2. _____
3. _____
_____
_____
_____

REFLECT
Which Core Desired Feeling seems farthest away? How do you feel about that?

SUNDAY April 21, 2019

Laylat al-Bara'at (Islam) | Easter Sunday (Christian)

What I will do to feel the way I want to feel

TO-DO ... make space for the light to enter

1. _____
2. _____
3. _____
_____
_____
_____

ENVISION
What would help you feel your Core Desired Feelings this week?

SOUL PROMPT I need to do less

Teach them how to Love.

SPACIOUS

MONDAY April 22, 2019 | *Earth Day*

MY CORE DESIRED FEELINGS

What I will do to feel the way I want to feel

SCHEDULE ... simplicity is freedom

: _____
: _____
: _____
: _____
: _____
: _____
: _____
: _____
: _____
: _____
: _____
: _____
: _____
: _____
: _____

TO-DO ... believe in yourself

1. _____
2. _____
3. _____
   _____
   _____
   _____

BODY & WELLNESS My body is telling me ...

DEVOTION I will light a candle for ...

NOT WORKING ... does it feel light or heavy?

STOP DOING ... speak up

GRATEFUL ... ask for more

Because ...

EASE

be done with enduring

TUESDAY April 23, 2019

MY CORE DESIRED FEELINGS

What I will do to feel the way I want to feel

SCHEDULE ... does it light you up?

: _____
: _____
: _____
: _____
: _____
: _____
: _____
: _____
: _____
: _____
: _____
: _____
: _____
: _____
: _____
: _____

TO-DO ... clarity creates simplicity

1. _____
2. _____
3. _____
   _____
   _____
   _____

BODY & WELLNESS I will respect my body ...

DEVOTION I will have faith that ...

NOT WORKING ... name it so you can change it

STOP DOING ... *No* makes way for *Yes*

GRATEFUL ... gratitude puts everything into perspective

Because ...

Love things just the way they are and watch what happens.

POWERFUL

WEDNESDAY April 24, 2019 | *Pluto stations Retrograde in Capricorn*

MY CORE DESIRED FEELINGS   *What I will do to feel the way I want to feel*

SCHEDULE ... joy expands time

: _____
: _____
: _____
: _____
: _____
: _____
: _____
: _____
: _____
: _____
: _____
: _____
: _____
: _____
: _____
: _____
: _____

TO-DO ... keep your soul on the agenda

1. _____
2. _____
3. _____
   _____
   _____
   _____

BODY & WELLNESS My body knows ...

DEVOTION Devotion creates miracles.

NOT WORKING ... don't hold back

STOP DOING ... clarity is power

GRATEFUL ... note WHY you're grateful   *Because ...*

JOY

What's driving your self-improvement?

THURSDAY April 25, 2019 | *ANZAC Day (AUS)*

MY CORE DESIRED FEELINGS   *What I will do to feel the way I want to feel*

SCHEDULE ... take up space

: _____
: _____
: _____
: _____
: _____
: _____
: _____
: _____
: _____
: _____
: _____
: _____
: _____
: _____
: _____
: _____

TO-DO ... make choices that liberate you

1. _____
2. _____
3. _____
_____
_____
_____

BODY & WELLNESS I will tend to my body ...

DEVOTION I will contemplate ...

NOT WORKING ... claim it. Tame it.

STOP DOING ... don't take any crap

GRATEFUL ... be a beacon of optimism   *Because ...*

Clarity creates simplicity.

DEEPLY LOVED

FRIDAY April 26, 2019

MY CORE DESIRED FEELINGS

What I will do to feel the way I want to feel

SCHEDULE ... what do you really want to happen?

: _____
: _____
: _____
: _____
: _____
: _____
: _____
: _____
: _____
: _____
: _____
: _____
: _____
: _____
: _____
: _____

TO-DO ... imagine

1. _____
2. _____
3. _____
   _____
   _____
   _____

BODY & WELLNESS I will nourish my body ...

DEVOTION I will pray for (who/what) ...

NOT WORKING ... feel free

STOP DOING ... freedom is your birthright

GRATEFUL ... specificity intensifies gratitude

Because ...

PLEASURE

If you want to increase your joy, deepen your devotion to knowing the Truth.

SATURDAY April 27, 2019
Passover ends - evening (Jewish holiday)

MY CORE DESIRED FEELINGS

SUNDAY April 28, 2019

What I will do to feel the way I want to feel

TO-DO ... what would be comforting?

1. _____
2. _____
3. _____
_____
_____
_____

TO-DO ... relax ... rebel ... rest

1. _____
2. _____
3. _____
_____
_____
_____

REFLECT
When you are feeling your CDFs, how does that help you be of more service to others?

ENVISION
How will you show up in the world as one of your CDFs?

SOUL PROMPT I identify with

Choose elegance.

VIBRANT

MONDAY April 29, 2019 | *Saturn stations Retrograde in Capricorn*

MY CORE DESIRED FEELINGS   *What I will do to feel the way I want to feel*

SCHEDULE ... leave room for magic

: _____
: _____
: _____
: _____
: _____
: _____
: _____
: _____
: _____
: _____
: _____
: _____
: _____
: _____
: _____
: _____

TO-DO ... prioritize pleasure

1. _____
2. _____
3. _____
   _____
   _____
   _____

BODY & WELLNESS My body helps me ...

DEVOTION My meditation will be ...

NOT WORKING ... does it feel light or heavy?

STOP DOING ... speak up

GRATEFUL ... ask for more   *Because ...*

EXPRESSIVE

Believe what you want—because what you believe will influence your future.

TUESDAY April 30, 2019

MY CORE DESIRED FEELINGS   *What I will do to feel the way I want to feel*

SCHEDULE ... work for Love

: _____
: _____
: _____
: _____
: _____
: _____
: _____
: _____
: _____
: _____
: _____
: _____
: _____
: _____
: _____
: _____

TO-DO ... do what lights you up

1. _____
2. _____
3. _____
   _____
   _____
   _____

BODY & WELLNESS My body is ...

DEVOTION I will dedicate this day to ...

NOT WORKING ... name it so you can change it

STOP DOING ... *No* makes way for *Yes*

GRATEFUL ... gratitude puts everything into perspective   *Because ...*

Things change—you change.

ATTENTIVE

THE PAST MONTH: Reflect. Clarify. Create.

EVERYDAY.

Small, deliberate actions—inspired by your Core Desired Feelings—create a life you love living. Big changes and choices may be called for, but it's how you show up every day that builds your strength.

MY CORE DESIRED FEELINGS
My CDFs are strongest in… I feel most aligned with… I'm moving toward…
I want to give more attention to…

MY GOALS & INTENTIONS
My goals are bringing my CDFs to life… I need to change up, refine or deepen…
To move closer to my goals & intentions I…

WHAT'S REALLY WORKING, YA!
I really felt [your CDF] when… This month I was so brilliant…
I created… I felt… I allowed… I accomplished…

WHAT NEEDS TO SHIFT
I felt disappointed… The challenge…

THE NEW MONTH: Envision. Intend. Energize.

WANT WHAT YOU WANT WITH ALL OF YOUR HEART.

"I want her to melt into me, like butter on toast. I want to observe her and walk around for the rest of my days with her encased in my skin. I want."
— Sara Gruen, *Water for Elephants*

HOW I WILL

be stronger… softer… more determined… less uptight… more flexible… less constricted… more open… less accommodating… more accommodating… less worried… more generous… less doubtful… more trusting… less punishing… more pleasure-creating… less fearful… more loving…

TO MOVE TOWARD MY GOALS & INTENTIONS…

MAY
2019

I am true, pure, generous radiance, streaming outward, always expanding. I seek to know more deeply, in every moment that: I am Light. Made of Light, surrounded by Light. I am Light. And so it is.

Imagine translucent light streaming through your crown chakra, filling your entire body, radiating out into every part of your life.

MONDAY	TUESDAY	WEDNESDAY
WEEK 18		**May Day/Beltane (Pagan)** — 1
Ramadan begins (Islam) | Early May Bank Holiday (UK) — 6 Mercury enters Taurus **WEEK 19**	7	8
13 **WEEK 20**	14	Venus enters Taurus Mars enters Cancer — 15
Victoria Day (CAN) — 20 **WEEK 21**	Sun enters Gemini Mercury enters Gemini — 21	22
Memorial Day (US) **Spring Bank Holiday (UK)** — 27 **WEEK 22**	28	29

THURSDAY	FRIDAY	SATURDAY	SUNDAY
2	3	● New Moon in Taurus 4	**Cinco de Mayo** 5
9	10	11	**Mother's Day (CAN, US)** 12
16	17	○ Full Moon in Scorpio 18	19
23	24	25	26
30	31		

MAY

WEDNESDAY May 1, 2019 | *May Day/Beltane (Pagan)*

MY CORE DESIRED FEELINGS   *What I will do to feel the way I want to feel*

SCHEDULE ... simplicity is freedom

: _____
: _____
: _____
: _____
: _____
: _____
: _____
: _____
: _____
: _____
: _____
: _____
: _____
: _____
: _____
: _____

TO-DO ... believe in yourself

1. _____
2. _____
3. _____
   _____
   _____
   _____

BODY & WELLNESS My body is telling me ...

DEVOTION I will light a candle for ...

NOT WORKING ... don't hold back

STOP DOING ... clarity is power

GRATEFUL ... note WHY you're grateful   *Because ...*

LIGHTNESS

Be kind. No matter what. (You can be kind and strong. You will need to be strong.)

THURSDAY May 2, 2019

MY CORE DESIRED FEELINGS

What I will do to feel the way I want to feel

SCHEDULE ... does it light you up?

: _____
: _____
: _____
: _____
: _____
: _____
: _____
: _____
: _____
: _____
: _____
: _____
: _____
: _____
: _____
: _____

TO-DO ... clarity creates simplicity

1. _____
2. _____
3. _____
   _____
   _____
   _____

BODY & WELLNESS I will respect my body ...

DEVOTION I will have faith that ...

NOT WORKING ... claim it. Tame it.

STOP DOING ... don't take any crap

GRATEFUL ... be a beacon of optimism

Because ...

Talk about how you feel.

EVER-EXPANDING

FRIDAY May 3, 2019

MY CORE DESIRED FEELINGS

What I will do to feel the way I want to feel

SCHEDULE ... joy expands time

: _____
: _____
: _____
: _____
: _____
: _____
: _____
: _____
: _____
: _____
: _____
: _____
: _____
: _____
: _____
: _____

TO-DO ... keep your soul on the agenda

1. _____
2. _____
3. _____
   _____
   _____
   _____

BODY & WELLNESS My body knows ...

DEVOTION Devotion creates miracles.

NOT WORKING ... feel free

STOP DOING ... freedom is your birthright

GRATEFUL ... specificity intensifies gratitude

Because ...

SWEET

The journey has to feel the way you want the destination to feel.

SATURDAY May 4, 2019
● *New Moon in Taurus*

MY CORE DESIRED FEELINGS

TO-DO ... visualize your ideal life

1. _____
2. _____
3. _____
   _____
   _____
   _____

REFLECT
Have a conversation with one of your CDFs, ask it to give you some guidance.

SUNDAY May 5, 2019
Cinco de Mayo

What I will do to feel the way I want to feel

TO-DO ... let it be easy

1. _____
2. _____
3. _____
   _____
   _____
   _____

ENVISION
What spaces or places embody your Core Desired Feelings?

SOUL PROMPT I feel vulnerable when

To innovate, you need to lighten your load. Constantly.

UNWAVERING

MONDAY May 6, 2019 | *Ramadan begins (Islam) | Early May Bank Holiday (UK) | Mercury enters Taurus*

MY CORE DESIRED FEELINGS

What I will do to feel the way I want to feel

SCHEDULE ... take up space

: _____
: _____
: _____
: _____
: _____
: _____
: _____
: _____
: _____
: _____
: _____
: _____
: _____
: _____
: _____
: _____

TO-DO ... make choices that liberate you

1. _____
2. _____
3. _____
   _____
   _____

BODY & WELLNESS I will tend to my body ...

DEVOTION I will contemplate ...

NOT WORKING ... does it feel light or heavy?

STOP DOING ... speak up

GRATEFUL ... ask for more

Because ...

SERENE

Speak clearly about your past.

TUESDAY May 7, 2019

MY CORE DESIRED FEELINGS

What I will do to feel the way I want to feel

SCHEDULE ... what do you really want to happen?

: _____
: _____
: _____
: _____
: _____
: _____
: _____
: _____
: _____
: _____
: _____
: _____
: _____
: _____
: _____
: _____
: _____

TO-DO ... imagine

1. _____
2. _____
3. _____
   _____
   _____
   _____

BODY & WELLNESS I will nourish my body ...

DEVOTION I will pray for (who/what) ...

NOT WORKING ... name it so you can change it

STOP DOING ... *No* makes way for *Yes*

GRATEFUL ... gratitude puts everything into perspective

Because ...

RESTED

Words protect.

WEDNESDAY May 8, 2019

MY CORE DESIRED FEELINGS

What I will do to feel the way I want to feel

SCHEDULE ... leave room for magic

: _____
: _____
: _____
: _____
: _____
: _____
: _____
: _____
: _____
: _____
: _____
: _____
: _____
: _____
: _____
: _____

TO-DO ... prioritize pleasure

1. _____
2. _____
3. _____
   _____
   _____
   _____

BODY & WELLNESS My body helps me ...

DEVOTION My meditation will be ...

NOT WORKING ... don't hold back

STOP DOING ... clarity is power

GRATEFUL ... note WHY you're grateful

Because ...

UNLIMITED

Keep your heart open and the answer will show up.

THURSDAY May 9, 2019

MY CORE DESIRED FEELINGS   *What I will do to feel the way I want to feel*

SCHEDULE ... work for Love

: _____
: _____
: _____
: _____
: _____
: _____
: _____
: _____
: _____
: _____
: _____
: _____
: _____
: _____
: _____
: _____

TO-DO ... do what lights you up

1. _____
2. _____
3. _____
   _____
   _____
   _____

BODY & WELLNESS My body is ...

DEVOTION I will dedicate this day to ...

NOT WORKING ... claim it. Tame it.

STOP DOING ... don't take any crap

GRATEFUL ... be a beacon of optimism   *Because ...*

You probably need more silence in your life.

COLORFUL

FRIDAY May 10, 2019

MY CORE DESIRED FEELINGS

What I will do to feel the way I want to feel

SCHEDULE ... simplicity is freedom

: _____
: _____
: _____
: _____
: _____
: _____
: _____
: _____
: _____
: _____
: _____
: _____
: _____
: _____
: _____
: _____

TO-DO ... believe in yourself

1. _____
2. _____
3. _____
   _____
   _____
   _____

BODY & WELLNESS My body is telling me ...

DEVOTION I will light a candle for ...

NOT WORKING ... feel free

STOP DOING ... freedom is your birthright

GRATEFUL ... specificity intensifies gratitude

Because ...

PERFECTION

Let your preferences evolve.

SATURDAY May 11, 2019

MY CORE DESIRED FEELINGS

SUNDAY May 12, 2019
Mother's Day (CAN, US)

What I will do to feel the way I want to feel

TO-DO ... make space for the light to enter

1. _____
2. _____
3. _____
_____
_____
_____

TO-DO ... what would be comforting?

1. _____
2. _____
3. _____
_____
_____
_____

REFLECT
Hands on your heart, eyes closed, recite your CDFs and see what images arise.

ENVISION
What Core Desired Feeling(s) need extra attention this week?

SOUL PROMPT I surrender to

Call your mother.

NURTURED

MONDAY May 13, 2019

MY CORE DESIRED FEELINGS

What I will do to feel the way I want to feel

SCHEDULE ... does it light you up?

: _____
: _____
: _____
: _____
: _____
: _____
: _____
: _____
: _____
: _____
: _____
: _____
: _____
: _____
: _____
: _____
: _____

TO-DO ... clarity creates simplicity

1. _____
2. _____
3. _____
   _____
   _____
   _____

BODY & WELLNESS I will respect my body ...

DEVOTION I will have faith that ...

NOT WORKING ... does it feel light or heavy?

STOP DOING ... speak up

GRATEFUL ... ask for more

Because ...

IN FLOW

It takes courage to change your beliefs.

TUESDAY May 14, 2019

MY CORE DESIRED FEELINGS   *What I will do to feel the way I want to feel*

SCHEDULE ... joy expands time

: _____
: _____
: _____
: _____
: _____
: _____
: _____
: _____
: _____
: _____
: _____
: _____
: _____
: _____
: _____

TO-DO ... keep your soul on the agenda

1. _____
2. _____
3. _____
   _____
   _____
   _____

BODY & WELLNESS My body knows ...

DEVOTION Devotion creates miracles.

NOT WORKING ... name it so you can change it

STOP DOING ... *No* makes way for *Yes*

GRATEFUL ... gratitude puts everything into perspective   *Because ...*

Small acts of freedom will really change your life.

LIGHT-HEARTED

WEDNESDAY May 15, 2019 | *Venus enters Taurus | Mars enters Cancer*

MY CORE DESIRED FEELINGS *What I will do to feel the way I want to feel*

SCHEDULE ... take up space

: _____
: _____
: _____
: _____
: _____
: _____
: _____
: _____
: _____
: _____
: _____
: _____
: _____
: _____
: _____
: _____

TO-DO ... make choices that liberate you

1. _____
2. _____
3. _____
   _____
   _____
   _____

BODY & WELLNESS I will tend to my body ...

DEVOTION I will contemplate ...

NOT WORKING ... don't hold back

STOP DOING ... clarity is power

GRATEFUL ... note WHY you're grateful   *Because ...*

SUPPORTED

Being discerning is not the same as being judgemental.

THURSDAY May 16, 2019

MY CORE DESIRED FEELINGS   *What I will do to feel the way I want to feel*

SCHEDULE ... what do you really want to happen?

: _____
: _____
: _____
: _____
: _____
: _____
: _____
: _____
: _____
: _____
: _____
: _____
: _____
: _____
: _____
: _____

TO-DO ... imagine

1. _____
2. _____
3. _____
_____
_____
_____

BODY & WELLNESS I will nourish my body ...

DEVOTION I will pray for (who/what) ...

NOT WORKING ... claim it. Tame it.

STOP DOING ... don't take any crap

GRATEFUL ... be a beacon of optimism   *Because ...*

Your freedom is good for all of us.

HOLISTIC

FRIDAY May 17, 2019

MY CORE DESIRED FEELINGS *What I will do to feel the way I want to feel*

SCHEDULE ... leave room for magic

: _____
: _____
: _____
: _____
: _____
: _____
: _____
: _____
: _____
: _____
: _____
: _____
: _____
: _____
: _____
: _____

TO-DO ... prioritize pleasure

1. _____
2. _____
3. _____
   _____
   _____
   _____

BODY & WELLNESS My body helps me ...

DEVOTION My meditation will be ...

NOT WORKING ... feel free

STOP DOING ... freedom is your birthright

GRATEFUL ... specificity intensifies gratitude   *Because ...*

TOUCHED

There's more where that came from.

SATURDAY May 18, 2019
○ *Full Moon in Scorpio*

MY CORE DESIRED FEELINGS

TO-DO ... relax ... rebel ... rest

1. _____
2. _____
3. _____
   _____
   _____
   _____

REFLECT
The Core Desired Feeling closest to my heart is...

SUNDAY May 19, 2019

What I will do to feel the way I want to feel

TO-DO ... visualize your ideal life

1. _____
2. _____
3. _____
   _____
   _____
   _____

ENVISION
How are your Core Desired Feelings experienced in your body?

SOUL PROMPT I've worked hard to

Declare your intentions.

NOURISHED

MONDAY May 20, 2019 | *Victoria Day (CAN)*

MY CORE DESIRED FEELINGS

What I will do to feel the way I want to feel

SCHEDULE ... work for Love

: _____
: _____
: _____
: _____
: _____
: _____
: _____
: _____
: _____
: _____
: _____
: _____
: _____
: _____
: _____
: _____

TO-DO ... do what lights you up

1. _____
2. _____
3. _____
   _____
   _____

BODY & WELLNESS My body is ...

DEVOTION I will dedicate this day to ...

NOT WORKING ... does it feel light or heavy?

STOP DOING ... speak up

GRATEFUL ... ask for more

Because ...

NURTURING

Use your freedom.

TUESDAY May 21, 2019 | *Sun enters Gemini | Mercury enters Gemini*

MY CORE DESIRED FEELINGS *What I will do to feel the way I want to feel*

SCHEDULE ... simplicity is freedom

:
:
:
:
:
:
:
:
:
:
:
:
:
:
:
:

TO-DO ... believe in yourself

1.
2.
3.

BODY & WELLNESS My body is telling me ...

DEVOTION I will light a candle for ...

NOT WORKING ... name it so you can change it

STOP DOING ... *No* makes way for *Yes*

GRATEFUL ... gratitude puts everything into perspective   *Because ...*

speak kindly to yourself

EMPOWERING

WEDNESDAY May 22, 2019

MY CORE DESIRED FEELINGS

What I will do to feel the way I want to feel

SCHEDULE ... does it light you up?

: _____
: _____
: _____
: _____
: _____
: _____
: _____
: _____
: _____
: _____
: _____
: _____
: _____
: _____
: _____
: _____

TO-DO ... clarity creates simplicity

1. _____
2. _____
3. _____
   _____
   _____
   _____

BODY & WELLNESS I will respect my body ...

DEVOTION I will have faith that ...

NOT WORKING ... don't hold back

STOP DOING ... clarity is power

GRATEFUL ... note WHY you're grateful

Because ...

ALIVE

The fewer expectations we carry, the more we have to offer.

THURSDAY May 23, 2019

MY CORE DESIRED FEELINGS

What I will do to feel the way I want to feel

SCHEDULE ... joy expands time

: _____
: _____
: _____
: _____
: _____
: _____
: _____
: _____
: _____
: _____
: _____
: _____
: _____
: _____
: _____
: _____
: _____

TO-DO ... keep your soul on the agenda

1. _____
2. _____
3. _____
   _____
   _____
   _____

BODY & WELLNESS My body knows ...

DEVOTION Devotion creates miracles.

NOT WORKING ... claim it. Tame it.

STOP DOING ... don't take any crap

GRATEFUL ... be a beacon of optimism

Because ...

May your beauty dawn on you.

DEEPLY

FRIDAY May 24, 2019

MY CORE DESIRED FEELINGS

What I will do to feel the way I want to feel

SCHEDULE ... take up space

: _____
: _____
: _____
: _____
: _____
: _____
: _____
: _____
: _____
: _____
: _____
: _____
: _____
: _____
: _____
: _____

TO-DO ... make choices that liberate you

1. _____
2. _____
3. _____
_____
_____
_____

BODY & WELLNESS I will tend to my body ...

DEVOTION I will contemplate ...

NOT WORKING ... feel free

STOP DOING ... freedom is your birthright

GRATEFUL ... specificity intensifies gratitude

Because ...

ROOTED

Surrender isn't about being passive. It's about being open.

SATURDAY May 25, 2019

MY CORE DESIRED FEELINGS

TO-DO ... let it be easy

1. _____
2. _____
3. _____
_____
_____
_____

REFLECT
A prayer: Thank you for the clarity and courage to make choices that favor my Core Desired Feelings.

SUNDAY May 26, 2019

What I will do to feel the way I want to feel

TO-DO ... make space for the light to enter

1. _____
2. _____
3. _____
_____
_____
_____

ENVISION
A prayer: Thank you for guiding me to express and experience my Core Desired Feelings.

SOUL PROMPT Three words that describe your anger

The paradox of manifestation: Be all in...and unattached.

INSPIRED

MONDAY May 27, 2019 | *Memorial Day (US) | Spring Bank Holiday (UK)*

MY CORE DESIRED FEELINGS   *What I will do to feel the way I want to feel*

SCHEDULE ... what do you really want to happen?

: _____
: _____
: _____
: _____
: _____
: _____
: _____
: _____
: _____
: _____
: _____
: _____
: _____
: _____
: _____

TO-DO ... imagine

1. _____
2. _____
3. _____
   _____
   _____
   _____

BODY & WELLNESS I will nourish my body ...

DEVOTION I will pray for (who/what) ...

NOT WORKING ... does it feel light or heavy?

STOP DOING ... speak up

GRATEFUL ... ask for more   *Because ...*

BRIGHT FAITH

Suspend judgment as a practice of faith.

TUESDAY May 28, 2019

MY CORE DESIRED FEELINGS   *What I will do to feel the way I want to feel*

SCHEDULE ... leave room for magic

: _____
: _____
: _____
: _____
: _____
: _____
: _____
: _____
: _____
: _____
: _____
: _____
: _____
: _____
: _____
: _____

TO-DO ... prioritize pleasure

1. _____
2. _____
3. _____
   _____
   _____
   _____

BODY & WELLNESS My body helps me ...

DEVOTION My meditation will be ...

NOT WORKING ... name it so you can change it

STOP DOING ... *No* makes way for *Yes*

GRATEFUL ... gratitude puts everything into perspective   *Because ...*

Prioritizing good sleep is good self love.

EARTHY

WEDNESDAY May 29, 2019

MY CORE DESIRED FEELINGS

What I will do to feel the way I want to feel

SCHEDULE ... work for Love

: _____
: _____
: _____
: _____
: _____
: _____
: _____
: _____
: _____
: _____
: _____
: _____
: _____
: _____
: _____
: _____

TO-DO ... do what lights you up

1. _____
2. _____
3. _____
   _____
   _____
   _____

BODY & WELLNESS My body is ...

DEVOTION I will dedicate this day to ...

NOT WORKING ... don't hold back

STOP DOING ... clarity is power

GRATEFUL ... note WHY you're grateful

Because ...

FRESH

We create our lives through loving.

THURSDAY May 30, 2019

MY CORE DESIRED FEELINGS					*What I will do to feel the way I want to feel*

SCHEDULE ... simplicity is freedom

   : _____
   : _____
   : _____
   : _____
   : _____
   : _____
   : _____
   : _____
   : _____
   : _____
   : _____
   : _____
   : _____
   : _____
   : _____
   : _____
   : _____

TO-DO ... believe in yourself

1. _____
2. _____
3. _____
_____
_____
_____

BODY & WELLNESS My body is telling me ...

DEVOTION I will light a candle for ...

NOT WORKING ... claim it. Tame it.

STOP DOING ... don't take any crap

GRATEFUL ... be a beacon of optimism			*Because ...*

BLISS

Joy is power.

FRIDAY May 31, 2019

MY CORE DESIRED FEELINGS

What I will do to feel the way I want to feel

SCHEDULE ... does it light you up?

: _____
: _____
: _____
: _____
: _____
: _____
: _____
: _____
: _____
: _____
: _____
: _____
: _____
: _____
: _____
: _____

TO-DO ... clarity creates simplicity

1. _____
2. _____
3. _____
   _____
   _____
   _____

BODY & WELLNESS I will respect my body ...

DEVOTION I will have faith that ...

NOT WORKING ... feel free

STOP DOING ... freedom is your birthright

GRATEFUL ... specificity intensifies gratitude

Because ...

GROOVIN

Believe in the power of beauty to heal.

IDEAS. DESIRES. WISDOM. ... keep your heart open

REPLENISHED

THE PAST MONTH: Reflect. Clarify. Create.

YOUR DESIRE IS A PRAYER

When you clarify, speak aloud, and give yourself permission to want what you want, you're sending the universe a clear signal that you're ready for fulfillment.

MY CORE DESIRED FEELINGS

My CDFs are strongest in… I feel most aligned with… I'm moving toward… I want to give more attention to…

MY GOALS & INTENTIONS

My goals are bringing my CDFs to life… I need to change up, refine or deepen… To move closer to my goals & intentions I…

WHAT'S REALLY WORKING, YA!

I really felt [your CDF] when… This month I was so brilliant… I created… I felt… I allowed… I accomplished…

WHAT NEEDS TO SHIFT

I felt disappointed… The challenge…

THE NEW MONTH: Envision. Intend. Energize.

SHARE YOUR STORY.
"We are volcanoes. When we women offer our experience as our truth, as human truth, all the maps change. There are new mountains."
— Ursula K. LeGuin

HOW I WILL
be stronger… softer… more determined… less uptight… more flexible… less constricted… more open… less accommodating… more accommodating… less worried… more generous… less doubtful… more trusting… less punishing… more pleasure-creating… less fearful… more loving…

TO MOVE TOWARD MY GOALS & INTENTIONS…

JUNE
2019

JUNE

I am the Love I seek, the Beauty I seek, the Truth I seek. I find myself in Love, Beauty and Truth.

Recite this when you're feeling the opposite of these positive states.

MONDAY	TUESDAY	WEDNESDAY
WEEK 22		
● New Moon in Gemini 3	**Ramadan ends (Islam)** 4 Mercury enters Cancer	**Eid al-Fitr (Islam)** 5
WEEK 23		
Shavuot ends - evening (Jewish holiday) **Queen's Birthday (AUS)** 10	11	12
WEEK 24		
○ Full Moon in Sagittarius 17	18	19
WEEK 25		
24	25	Mercury enters Leo 26
WEEK 26		

THURSDAY	FRIDAY	SATURDAY	SUNDAY
		Laylat al-Qadr (Islam) 1	2
6	7	**Shavuot begins - evening (Jewish holiday)** 8 **Queen's Birthday (UK)** Venus enters Gemini	9
13	14	15	**Father's Day** 16
20	**Summer Solstice/ Litha (Pagan)** 21 **National Indigenous Peoples Day (CAN)** Sun enters Cancer Neptune stations Retrograde in Pisces	22	23
27	28	29	30

JUNE

SATURDAY June 1, 2019
Laylat al-Qadr (Islam)

MY CORE DESIRED FEELINGS

TO-DO ... what would be comforting?

1. _____
2. _____
3. _____
_____
_____
_____

REFLECT
What Core Desired Feeling felt most alive in your life? Why/how?

SUNDAY June 2, 2019

What I will do to feel the way I want to feel

TO-DO ... relax ... rebel ... rest

1. _____
2. _____
3. _____
_____
_____
_____

ENVISION
What rituals support your Core Desired Feelings?

SOUL PROMPT I'm curious about

CHERISHED

Restraint isn't always restrictive.

MONDAY June 3, 2019 | ● *New Moon in Gemini*

MY CORE DESIRED FEELINGS   *What I will do to feel the way I want to feel*

SCHEDULE ... joy expands time

: _____
: _____
: _____
: _____
: _____
: _____
: _____
: _____
: _____
: _____
: _____
: _____
: _____
: _____
: _____
: _____

TO-DO ... keep your soul on the agenda

1. _____
2. _____
3. _____
   _____
   _____
   _____

BODY & WELLNESS My body knows ...

DEVOTION Devotion creates miracles.

NOT WORKING ... does it feel light or heavy?

STOP DOING ... speak up

GRATEFUL ... ask for more   *Because ...*

What would your life be like if you only did what was easy?

SOUL

TUESDAY June 4, 2019 | *Ramadan ends (Islam) | Mercury enters Cancer*

MY CORE DESIRED FEELINGS *What I will do to feel the way I want to feel*

SCHEDULE ... take up space

: _____
: _____
: _____
: _____
: _____
: _____
: _____
: _____
: _____
: _____
: _____
: _____
: _____
: _____
: _____
: _____

TO-DO ... make choices that liberate you

1. _____
2. _____
3. _____
   _____
   _____
   _____

BODY & WELLNESS I will tend to my body ...

DEVOTION I will contemplate ...

NOT WORKING ... name it so you can change it

STOP DOING ... *No* makes way for *Yes*

GRATEFUL ... gratitude puts everything into perspective   *Because ...*

BLISSED OUT

Thank you for not thinking that integrity is an inconvenience.

WEDNESDAY June 5, 2019 | *Eid al-Fitr (Islam)*

MY CORE DESIRED FEELINGS

What I will do to feel the way I want to feel

SCHEDULE ... what do you really want to happen?

: _____
: _____
: _____
: _____
: _____
: _____
: _____
: _____
: _____
: _____
: _____
: _____
: _____
: _____
: _____
: _____
: _____

TO-DO ... imagine

1. _____
2. _____
3. _____
_____
_____
_____

BODY & WELLNESS I will nourish my body ...

DEVOTION I will pray for (who/what) ...

NOT WORKING ... don't hold back

STOP DOING ... clarity is power

GRATEFUL ... note WHY you're grateful

Because ...

Cynicism is a toxic substance.

ELECTRIC

THURSDAY June 6, 2019

MY CORE DESIRED FEELINGS

What I will do to feel the way I want to feel

SCHEDULE ... leave room for magic

: _____
: _____
: _____
: _____
: _____
: _____
: _____
: _____
: _____
: _____
: _____
: _____
: _____
: _____
: _____
: _____

TO-DO ... prioritize pleasure

1. _____
2. _____
3. _____
   _____
   _____
   _____

BODY & WELLNESS My body helps me ...

DEVOTION My meditation will be ...

NOT WORKING ... claim it. Tame it.

STOP DOING ... don't take any crap

GRATEFUL ... be a beacon of optimism

Because ...

STRENGTH

Peace of mind is power.

FRIDAY June 7, 2019

MY CORE DESIRED FEELINGS   *What I will do to feel the way I want to feel*

SCHEDULE ... work for Love

: _____
: _____
: _____
: _____
: _____
: _____
: _____
: _____
: _____
: _____
: _____
: _____
: _____
: _____
: _____
: _____
: _____

TO-DO ... do what lights you up

1. _____
2. _____
3. _____
_____
_____
_____

BODY & WELLNESS My body is ...

DEVOTION I will dedicate this day to ...

NOT WORKING ... feel free

STOP DOING ... freedom is your birthright

GRATEFUL ... specificity intensifies gratitude   *Because ...*

Faith is the "work" in "Light work"

LUXURIOUS

SATURDAY June 8, 2019

Shavuot begins - evening (Jewish holiday)
Queen's Birthday (UK) | Venus enters Gemini

MY CORE DESIRED FEELINGS

TO-DO ... visualize your ideal life

1. _____
2. _____
3. _____
   _____
   _____
   _____

REFLECT
Which Core Desired Feeling seems farthest away? How do you feel about that?

SUNDAY June 9, 2019

What I will do to feel the way I want to feel

TO-DO ... let it be easy

1. _____
2. _____
3. _____
   _____
   _____
   _____

ENVISION
What would help you feel your Core Desired Feelings this week?

SOUL PROMPT I am trying to impress

ARTISTIC

The journey to sovereignty is usually pretty messy.

MONDAY June 10, 2019 | *Shavuot ends - evening (Jewish holiday) | Queen's Birthday (AUS)*

MY CORE DESIRED FEELINGS*What I will do to feel the way I want to feel*

SCHEDULE ... simplicity is freedom

   : _____

   : _____

   : _____

   : _____

   : _____

   : _____

   : _____

   : _____

   : _____

   : _____

   : _____

   : _____

   : _____

   : _____

   : _____

TO-DO ... believe in yourself

1. _____
2. _____
3. _____

_____

_____

_____

BODY & WELLNESS My body is telling me ...

DEVOTION I will light a candle for ...

NOT WORKING ... does it feel light or heavy?

STOP DOING ... speak up

GRATEFUL ... ask for more*Because ...*

Use your voice.

SPARK

TUESDAY June 11, 2019

MY CORE DESIRED FEELINGS

What I will do to feel the way I want to feel

SCHEDULE ... does it light you up?

: _____
: _____
: _____
: _____
: _____
: _____
: _____
: _____
: _____
: _____
: _____
: _____
: _____
: _____
: _____
: _____

TO-DO ... clarity creates simplicity

1. _____
2. _____
3. _____
_____
_____
_____

BODY & WELLNESS I will respect my body ...

DEVOTION I will have faith that ...

NOT WORKING ... name it so you can change it

STOP DOING ... *No* makes way for *Yes*

GRATEFUL ... gratitude puts everything into perspective

Because ...

VICTORIOUS

Joy is what happens when you make contact with your Soul.

WEDNESDAY June 12, 2019

MY CORE DESIRED FEELINGS

What I will do to feel the way I want to feel

SCHEDULE ... joy expands time

___ : _____
___ : _____
___ : _____
___ : _____
___ : _____
___ : _____
___ : _____
___ : _____
___ : _____
___ : _____
___ : _____
___ : _____
___ : _____
___ : _____
___ : _____
___ : _____

TO-DO ... keep your soul on the agenda

1. _____
2. _____
3. _____
_____
_____
_____

BODY & WELLNESS My body knows ...

DEVOTION Devotion creates miracles.

NOT WORKING ... don't hold back

STOP DOING ... clarity is power

GRATEFUL ... note WHY you're grateful

Because ...

IRRESISTIBLE

You are never the only one.

THURSDAY June 13, 2019

MY CORE DESIRED FEELINGS

What I will do to feel the way I want to feel

SCHEDULE ... take up space

: _____
: _____
: _____
: _____
: _____
: _____
: _____
: _____
: _____
: _____
: _____
: _____
: _____
: _____
: _____
: _____

TO-DO ... make choices that liberate you

1. _____
2. _____
3. _____
   _____
   _____
   _____

BODY & WELLNESS I will tend to my body ...

DEVOTION I will contemplate ...

NOT WORKING ... claim it. Tame it.

STOP DOING ... don't take any crap

GRATEFUL ... be a beacon of optimism

Because ...

COMPLETE

May your pure Faith light the way.

FRIDAY June 14, 2019

MY CORE DESIRED FEELINGS

What I will do to feel the way I want to feel

SCHEDULE ... what do you really want to happen?

: _____
: _____
: _____
: _____
: _____
: _____
: _____
: _____
: _____
: _____
: _____
: _____
: _____
: _____
: _____
: _____
: _____

TO-DO ... imagine

1. _____
2. _____
3. _____
   _____
   _____
   _____

BODY & WELLNESS I will nourish my body ...

DEVOTION I will pray for (who/what) ...

NOT WORKING ... feel free

STOP DOING ... freedom is your birthright

GRATEFUL ... specificity intensifies gratitude

Because ...

ILLUMIN-ABLE

Your self-expression is a great service to the world.

SATURDAY June 15, 2019

MY CORE DESIRED FEELINGS

TO-DO ... make space for the light to enter

1. _____
2. _____
3. _____
_____
_____
_____

REFLECT
When you are feeling your CDFs, how does that help you be of more service to others?

SUNDAY June 16, 2019
Father's Day

What I will do to feel the way I want to feel

TO-DO ... what would be comforting?

1. _____
2. _____
3. _____
_____
_____
_____

ENVISION
How will you show up in the world as one of your CDFs?

SOUL PROMPT I must

SENSUAL

Think of resentment as a mega-watt STOP sign. And stop.

MONDAY June 17, 2019 | ○ *Full Moon in Sagittarius*

MY CORE DESIRED FEELINGS   *What I will do to feel the way I want to feel*

SCHEDULE ... leave room for magic   **TO-DO** ... prioritize pleasure

: _____   1. _____
: _____   2. _____
: _____   3. _____
: _____   _____
: _____   _____
: _____   _____
: _____   **BODY & WELLNESS** My body helps me ...
: _____
: _____   **DEVOTION** My meditation will be ...
: _____
: _____   **NOT WORKING** ... does it feel light or heavy?
: _____
: _____
: _____   **STOP DOING** ... speak up
: _____
: _____

GRATEFUL ... ask for more   *Because ...*

Dedicate your day to someone.   GROWING

TUESDAY June 18, 2019

MY CORE DESIRED FEELINGS

What I will do to feel the way I want to feel

SCHEDULE ... work for Love

: _____
: _____
: _____
: _____
: _____
: _____
: _____
: _____
: _____
: _____
: _____
: _____
: _____
: _____
: _____
: _____
: _____

TO-DO ... do what lights you up

1. _____
2. _____
3. _____
   _____
   _____

BODY & WELLNESS My body is ...

DEVOTION I will dedicate this day to ...

NOT WORKING ... name it so you can change it

STOP DOING ... *No* makes way for *Yes*

GRATEFUL ... gratitude puts everything into perspective

Because ...

HOLY

Let there be space between you and your wish so fulfillment can pour in.

WEDNESDAY June 19, 2019

MY CORE DESIRED FEELINGS

What I will do to feel the way I want to feel

SCHEDULE ... simplicity is freedom

: _____
: _____
: _____
: _____
: _____
: _____
: _____
: _____
: _____
: _____
: _____
: _____
: _____
: _____
: _____
: _____

TO-DO ... believe in yourself

1. _____
2. _____
3. _____
   _____
   _____
   _____

BODY & WELLNESS My body is telling me ...

DEVOTION I will light a candle for ...

NOT WORKING ... don't hold back

STOP DOING ... clarity is power

GRATEFUL ... note WHY you're grateful

Because ...

Discernment is crucial to spiritual freedom.

PLAYFUL

THURSDAY June 20, 2019

MY CORE DESIRED FEELINGS

What I will do to feel the way I want to feel

SCHEDULE ... does it light you up?

: _____
: _____
: _____
: _____
: _____
: _____
: _____
: _____
: _____
: _____
: _____
: _____
: _____
: _____
: _____

TO-DO ... clarity creates simplicity

1. _____
2. _____
3. _____
   _____
   _____
   _____

BODY & WELLNESS I will respect my body ...

DEVOTION I will have faith that ...

NOT WORKING ... claim it. Tame it.

STOP DOING ... don't take any crap

GRATEFUL ... be a beacon of optimism

Because ...

LAVISH

Self-deception is part of self-discovery.

FRIDAY June 21, 2019 | *Summer Solstice/Litha (Pagan) | National Indigenous Peoples Day (CAN)*
Sun enters Cancer | Neptune stations Retrograde in Pisces

MY CORE DESIRED FEELINGS   *What I will do to feel the way I want to feel*

SCHEDULE ... joy expands time

: _____
: _____
: _____
: _____
: _____
: _____
: _____
: _____
: _____
: _____
: _____
: _____
: _____
: _____
: _____
: _____
: _____

TO-DO ... keep your soul on the agenda

1. _____
2. _____
3. _____
   _____
   _____
   _____

BODY & WELLNESS My body knows ...

DEVOTION Devotion creates miracles.

NOT WORKING ... feel free

STOP DOING ... freedom is your birthright

GRATEFUL ... specificity intensifies gratitude   *Because ...*

Devotion cures.

DEDICATED

SATURDAY June 22, 2019

MY CORE DESIRED FEELINGS

TO-DO ... relax ... rebel ... rest

1. _____
2. _____
3. _____

_____
_____
_____

REFLECT
Have a conversation with one of your CDFs, ask it to give you some guidance.

SUNDAY June 23, 2019

What I will do to feel the way I want to feel

TO-DO ... visualize your ideal life

1. _____
2. _____
3. _____

_____
_____
_____

ENVISION
What spaces or places embody your Core Desired Feelings?

SOUL PROMPT One word to describe your work in the world

DIVINELY-GUIDED

Take back what's yours.

MONDAY June 24, 2019

MY CORE DESIRED FEELINGS

What I will do to feel the way I want to feel

SCHEDULE ... take up space

: _____
: _____
: _____
: _____
: _____
: _____
: _____
: _____
: _____
: _____
: _____
: _____
: _____
: _____
: _____
: _____
: _____

TO-DO ... make choices that liberate you

1. _____
2. _____
3. _____
_____
_____
_____

BODY & WELLNESS I will tend to my body ...

DEVOTION I will contemplate ...

NOT WORKING ... does it feel light or heavy?

STOP DOING ... speak up

GRATEFUL ... ask for more

Because ...

Having high standards works wonders.

DISCIPLINED

TUESDAY June 25, 2019

MY CORE DESIRED FEELINGS

What I will do to feel the way I want to feel

SCHEDULE ... what do you really want to happen?

: _____
: _____
: _____
: _____
: _____
: _____
: _____
: _____
: _____
: _____
: _____
: _____
: _____
: _____
: _____
: _____
: _____

TO-DO ... imagine

1. _____
2. _____
3. _____
_____
_____
_____

BODY & WELLNESS I will nourish my body ...

DEVOTION I will pray for (who/what) ...

NOT WORKING ... name it so you can change it

STOP DOING ... *No* makes way for *Yes*

GRATEFUL ... gratitude puts everything into perspective

Because ...

ANCHORED

Love the Truth into being.

WEDNESDAY June 26, 2019 | *Mercury enters Leo*

MY CORE DESIRED FEELINGS   *What I will do to feel the way I want to feel*

SCHEDULE ... leave room for magic

__ : _____

__ : _____

__ : _____

__ : _____

__ : _____

__ : _____

__ : _____

__ : _____

__ : _____

__ : _____

__ : _____

__ : _____

__ : _____

__ : _____

__ : _____

TO-DO ... prioritize pleasure

1. _____

2. _____

3. _____

BODY & WELLNESS My body helps me ...

DEVOTION My meditation will be ...

NOT WORKING ... don't hold back

STOP DOING ... clarity is power

GRATEFUL ... note WHY you're grateful   *Because ...*

AT EASE

Be the anomaly.

THURSDAY June 27, 2019

MY CORE DESIRED FEELINGS

What I will do to feel the way I want to feel

SCHEDULE ... work for Love

: _____
: _____
: _____
: _____
: _____
: _____
: _____
: _____
: _____
: _____
: _____
: _____
: _____
: _____
: _____
: _____
: _____

TO-DO ... do what lights you up

1. _____
2. _____
3. _____
   _____
   _____
   _____

BODY & WELLNESS My body is ...

DEVOTION I will dedicate this day to ...

NOT WORKING ... claim it. Tame it.

STOP DOING ... don't take any crap

GRATEFUL ... be a beacon of optimism

Because ...

FIERCE LOVE

Tend your insight like a fire.

FRIDAY June 28, 2019

MY CORE DESIRED FEELINGS

What I will do to feel the way I want to feel

SCHEDULE ... simplicity is freedom

_ : _____
_ : _____
_ : _____
_ : _____
_ : _____
_ : _____
_ : _____
_ : _____
_ : _____
_ : _____
_ : _____
_ : _____
_ : _____
_ : _____
_ : _____
_ : _____

TO-DO ... believe in yourself

1. _____
2. _____
3. _____
_____
_____
_____

BODY & WELLNESS My body is telling me ...

DEVOTION I will light a candle for ...

NOT WORKING ... feel free

STOP DOING ... freedom is your birthright

GRATEFUL ... specificity intensifies gratitude

Because ...

the universe cannot resist authenticity

PRESENT

SATURDAY June 29, 2019

MY CORE DESIRED FEELINGS

TO-DO ... let it be easy

1. _____
2. _____
3. _____
_____
_____
_____

REFLECT
Hands on your heart, eyes closed, recite your CDFs and see what images arise.

SOUL PROMPT I am burning

VIVACIOUS

SUNDAY June 30, 2019

What I will do to feel the way I want to feel

TO-DO ... make space for the light to enter

1. _____
2. _____
3. _____
_____
_____
_____

ENVISION
What Core Desired Feeling(s) need extra attention this week?

You are healing.

IDEAS. DESIRES. WISDOM. ... your desires are sacred

If you declare that you'll figure it out, the possibilities are endless.

THE PAST MONTH: Reflect. Clarify. Create.

LOOK YOUR DESIRE IN THE EYE.

When you examine how you *really want to feel*, something phenomenal happens: you see your current situation more clearly—what needs to change, as well as everything that you're incredibly grateful for. And you also take a step closer to your potential.

MY CORE DESIRED FEELINGS

My CDFs are strongest in… I feel most aligned with… I'm moving toward…
I want to give more attention to…

MY GOALS & INTENTIONS

My goals are bringing my CDFs to life… I need to change up, refine or deepen…
To move closer to my goals & intentions I…

WHAT'S REALLY WORKING, YA!

I really felt [your CDF] when… This month I was so brilliant…
I created… I felt… I allowed… I accomplished…

WHAT NEEDS TO SHIFT

I felt disappointed… The challenge…

THE NEW MONTH: Envision. Intend. Energize.

ALL MAKING IS A MESS UNTIL IT IS BEAUTIFUL.

"We don't call it anxiety. We call it inspiration—the
part between having an idea and desperation."
— Margaret Atwood

HOW I WILL

be stronger… softer… more determined… less uptight… more flexible… less constricted… more open… less accommodating… more accommodating… less worried… more generous… less doubtful… more trusting… less punishing… more pleasure-creating… less fearful… more loving…

TO MOVE TOWARD MY GOALS & INTENTIONS…

JULY
2019

Om shrim maha Lakshmiyei swaha (Phonetically; Om shreem mah-ha lahk-shmee-yay swah-hah)

"Om and salutations to she who manifests every kind of abundance." This is the mantra to Lakshmi, goddess of prosperity, purity, generosity.

MONDAY	TUESDAY	WEDNESDAY
Canada Day — Mars enters Leo — 1	● New Moon in Cancer - Total Solar Eclipse — 2	Venus enters Cancer — 3
WEEK 27		
8	9	10
WEEK 28		
15	○ Full Moon in Capricorn - Partial Lunar Eclipse — 16	17
WEEK 29		
Sun enters Leo — 22	23	24
WEEK 30		
29	30	● New Moon in Leo — Mercury stations Direct in Cancer — 31
WEEK 31		

THURSDAY	FRIDAY	SATURDAY	SUNDAY
Independence Day (US) 4	5	6	Mercury stations Retrograde in Leo 7
11	12	13	14
18	19	20	21
25	26	Venus enters Leo 27	28

JULY

MONDAY July 1, 2019 | *Canada Day* | Mars enters Leo

MY CORE DESIRED FEELINGS   *What I will do to feel the way I want to feel*

SCHEDULE ... does it light you up?

: _____
: _____
: _____
: _____
: _____
: _____
: _____
: _____
: _____
: _____
: _____
: _____
: _____
: _____
: _____
: _____

TO-DO ... clarity creates simplicity

1. _____
2. _____
3. _____
_____
_____
_____

BODY & WELLNESS I will respect my body ...

DEVOTION I will have faith that ...

NOT WORKING ... does it feel light or heavy?

STOP DOING ... speak up

GRATEFUL ... ask for more   *Because ...*

TRUTH

Cultivate more tenderness.

TUESDAY July 2, 2019 | ● *New Moon in Cancer - Total Solar Eclipse*

MY CORE DESIRED FEELINGS   *What I will do to feel the way I want to feel*

SCHEDULE ... joy expands time

: _____
: _____
: _____
: _____
: _____
: _____
: _____
: _____
: _____
: _____
: _____
: _____
: _____
: _____
: _____
: _____

TO-DO ... keep your soul on the agenda

1. _____
2. _____
3. _____
   _____
   _____
   _____

BODY & WELLNESS My body knows ...

DEVOTION Devotion creates miracles.

NOT WORKING ... name it so you can change it

STOP DOING ... *No* makes way for *Yes*

GRATEFUL ... gratitude puts everything into perspective   *Because ...*

Don't say it if you don't mean it.

JOY

WEDNESDAY July 3, 2019 | *Venus enters Cancer*

MY CORE DESIRED FEELINGS

What I will do to feel the way I want to feel

SCHEDULE ... take up space

: _____
: _____
: _____
: _____
: _____
: _____
: _____
: _____
: _____
: _____
: _____
: _____
: _____
: _____
: _____

TO-DO ... make choices that liberate you

1. _____
2. _____
3. _____
   _____
   _____
   _____

BODY & WELLNESS I will tend to my body ...

DEVOTION I will contemplate ...

NOT WORKING ... don't hold back

STOP DOING ... clarity is power

GRATEFUL ... note WHY you're grateful

Because ...

CELEBRATED

Settling for crumbs doesn't keep you fed—it keeps you starving.

THURSDAY July 4, 2019 | *Independence Day (US)*

MY CORE DESIRED FEELINGS   *What I will do to feel the way I want to feel*

SCHEDULE ... what do you really want to happen?

: _____
: _____
: _____
: _____
: _____
: _____
: _____
: _____
: _____
: _____
: _____
: _____
: _____
: _____
: _____
: _____
: _____

TO-DO ... imagine

1. _____
2. _____
3. _____
   _____
   _____
   _____

BODY & WELLNESS I will nourish my body ...

DEVOTION I will pray for (who/what) ...

NOT WORKING ... claim it. Tame it.

STOP DOING ... don't take any crap

GRATEFUL ... be a beacon of optimism   *Because ...*

DARING

Doing The Right Thing is often an imposition. Do it anyway.

FRIDAY July 5, 2019

MY CORE DESIRED FEELINGS   *What I will do to feel the way I want to feel*

SCHEDULE ... leave room for magic

: _____
: _____
: _____
: _____
: _____
: _____
: _____
: _____
: _____
: _____
: _____
: _____
: _____
: _____
: _____
: _____

TO-DO ... prioritize pleasure

1. _____
2. _____
3. _____
   _____
   _____
   _____

BODY & WELLNESS My body helps me ...

DEVOTION My meditation will be ...

NOT WORKING ... feel free

STOP DOING ... freedom is your birthright

GRATEFUL ... specificity intensifies gratitude   *Because ...*

SURE

Your scars are someone else's signs of hope.

SATURDAY July 6, 2019

MY CORE DESIRED FEELINGS

татн

TO-DO ... what would be comforting?

1. _____
2. _____
3. _____
   _____
   _____
   _____

REFLECT
The Core Desired Feeling closest to my heart is...

SOUL PROMPT I feel the most free when

SUNDAY July 7, 2019
Mercury stations Retrograde in Leo

What I will do to feel the way I want to feel

TO-DO ... relax ... rebel ... rest

1. _____
2. _____
3. _____
   _____
   _____
   _____

ENVISION
How are your Core Desired Feelings experienced in your body?

Disappointments can be openings.

OTHER-WORLDLY

MONDAY July 8, 2019

MY CORE DESIRED FEELINGS   *What I will do to feel the way I want to feel*

SCHEDULE ... work for Love

: _____
: _____
: _____
: _____
: _____
: _____
: _____
: _____
: _____
: _____
: _____
: _____
: _____
: _____
: _____

TO-DO ... do what lights you up

1. _____
2. _____
3. _____
   _____
   _____

BODY & WELLNESS My body is ...

DEVOTION I will dedicate this day to ...

NOT WORKING ... does it feel light or heavy?

STOP DOING ... speak up

GRATEFUL ... ask for more   *Because ...*

ENCHANT-
MENT

Change the game.

TUESDAY July 9, 2019

MY CORE DESIRED FEELINGS   *What I will do to feel the way I want to feel*

SCHEDULE ... simplicity is freedom   **TO-DO** ... believe in yourself

: _____   1. _____
: _____   2. _____
: _____   3. _____
: _____   _____
: _____   _____
: _____   _____
: _____   **BODY & WELLNESS** My body is telling me ...
: _____
: _____   **DEVOTION** I will light a candle for ...
: _____
: _____
: _____   **NOT WORKING** ... name it so you can change it
: _____
: _____
: _____   **STOP DOING** ... *No* makes way for *Yes*
: _____
: _____

GRATEFUL ... gratitude puts everything into perspective   *Because ...*

Do it for your own fulfilment.

COSMIC

WEDNESDAY July 10, 2019

MY CORE DESIRED FEELINGS

What I will do to feel the way I want to feel

SCHEDULE ... does it light you up?

: _____
: _____
: _____
: _____
: _____
: _____
: _____
: _____
: _____
: _____
: _____
: _____
: _____
: _____
: _____
: _____

TO-DO ... clarity creates simplicity

1. _____
2. _____
3. _____
   _____
   _____
   _____

BODY & WELLNESS I will respect my body ...

DEVOTION I will have faith that ...

NOT WORKING ... don't hold back

STOP DOING ... clarity is power

GRATEFUL ... note WHY you're grateful

Because ...

FERVENT

dream of being amazed

THURSDAY July 11, 2019

MY CORE DESIRED FEELINGS   *What I will do to feel the way I want to feel*

SCHEDULE ... joy expands time

: _____
: _____
: _____
: _____
: _____
: _____
: _____
: _____
: _____
: _____
: _____
: _____
: _____
: _____
: _____
: _____
: _____

TO-DO ... keep your soul on the agenda

1. _____
2. _____
3. _____
   _____
   _____
   _____

BODY & WELLNESS My body knows ...

DEVOTION Devotion creates miracles.

NOT WORKING ... claim it. Tame it.

STOP DOING ... don't take any crap

GRATEFUL ... be a beacon of optimism   *Because ...*

RADIANT

When faced with a choice between a deadline and a friend, almost always choose the friend.

FRIDAY July 12, 2019

MY CORE DESIRED FEELINGS

What I will do to feel the way I want to feel

SCHEDULE ... take up space

: _____
: _____
: _____
: _____
: _____
: _____
: _____
: _____
: _____
: _____
: _____
: _____
: _____
: _____
: _____
: _____

TO-DO ... make choices that liberate you

1. _____
2. _____
3. _____
   _____
   _____
   _____

BODY & WELLNESS I will tend to my body ...

DEVOTION I will contemplate ...

NOT WORKING ... feel free

STOP DOING ... freedom is your birthright

GRATEFUL ... specificity intensifies gratitude

Because ...

CURIOUS

Pray ceaselessly.

SATURDAY July 13, 2019

MY CORE DESIRED FEELINGS

TO-DO ... visualize your ideal life

1. _____
2. _____
3. _____
   _____
   _____
   _____

REFLECT
A prayer: Thank you for the clarity and courage to make choices that favor my Core Desired Feelings.

SUNDAY July 14, 2019

What I will do to feel the way I want to feel

TO-DO ... let it be easy

1. _____
2. _____
3. _____
   _____
   _____
   _____

ENVISION
A prayer: Thank you for guiding me to express and experience my Core Desired Feelings.

SOUL PROMPT I'm a really good

Replay your breakthrough experiences.

INSTINCTIVE

MONDAY July 15, 2019

MY CORE DESIRED FEELINGS

What I will do to feel the way I want to feel

SCHEDULE ... what do you really want to happen?

: _____
: _____
: _____
: _____
: _____
: _____
: _____
: _____
: _____
: _____
: _____
: _____
: _____
: _____
: _____
: _____

TO-DO ... imagine

1. _____
2. _____
3. _____
   _____
   _____

BODY & WELLNESS I will nourish my body ...

DEVOTION I will pray for (who/what) ...

NOT WORKING ... does it feel light or heavy?

STOP DOING ... speak up

GRATEFUL ... ask for more

Because ...

IN AWE

After logic... meditate.

TUESDAY July 16, 2019 | ○ *Full Moon in Capricorn - Partial Lunar Eclipse*

MY CORE DESIRED FEELINGS   *What I will do to feel the way I want to feel*

SCHEDULE ... leave room for magic

: _____
: _____
: _____
: _____
: _____
: _____
: _____
: _____
: _____
: _____
: _____
: _____
: _____
: _____
: _____
: _____

TO-DO ... prioritize pleasure

1. _____
2. _____
3. _____
   _____
   _____
   _____

BODY & WELLNESS My body helps me ...

DEVOTION My meditation will be ...

NOT WORKING ... name it so you can change it

STOP DOING ... *No* makes way for *Yes*

GRATEFUL ... gratitude puts everything into perspective   *Because ...*

If you want to do great things, striving for "balance" is a losing game.

FAITH

WEDNESDAY July 17, 2019

MY CORE DESIRED FEELINGS

What I will do to feel the way I want to feel

SCHEDULE ... work for Love

: _____
: _____
: _____
: _____
: _____
: _____
: _____
: _____
: _____
: _____
: _____
: _____
: _____
: _____
: _____
: _____

TO-DO ... do what lights you up

1. _____
2. _____
3. _____
_____
_____
_____

BODY & WELLNESS My body is ...

DEVOTION I will dedicate this day to ...

NOT WORKING ... don't hold back

STOP DOING ... clarity is power

GRATEFUL ... note WHY you're grateful

Because ...

BRIGHT

Trust helps the insights to surface.

THURSDAY July 18, 2019

MY CORE DESIRED FEELINGS — *What I will do to feel the way I want to feel*

SCHEDULE ... simplicity is freedom

: _____
: _____
: _____
: _____
: _____
: _____
: _____
: _____
: _____
: _____
: _____
: _____
: _____
: _____
: _____
: _____
: _____

TO-DO ... believe in yourself

1. _____
2. _____
3. _____
   _____
   _____
   _____

BODY & WELLNESS My body is telling me ...

DEVOTION I will light a candle for ...

NOT WORKING ... claim it. Tame it.

STOP DOING ... don't take any crap

GRATEFUL ... be a beacon of optimism   *Because ...*

Ask your Soul what it sees.

BLOSSOMING

FRIDAY July 19, 2019

MY CORE DESIRED FEELINGS

What I will do to feel the way I want to feel

SCHEDULE ... does it light you up?

: _____
: _____
: _____
: _____
: _____
: _____
: _____
: _____
: _____
: _____
: _____
: _____
: _____
: _____
: _____
: _____
: _____

TO-DO ... clarity creates simplicity

1. _____
2. _____
3. _____
   _____
   _____
   _____

BODY & WELLNESS I will respect my body ...

DEVOTION I will have faith that ...

NOT WORKING ... feel free

STOP DOING ... freedom is your birthright

GRATEFUL ... specificity intensifies gratitude

Because ...

ENERGETIC

Change often triggers guilt.

SATURDAY July 20, 2019

MY CORE DESIRED FEELINGS

TO-DO ... make space for the light to enter

1. _____
2. _____
3. _____
_____
_____
_____

REFLECT
What Core Desired Feeling felt most alive in your life? Why/how?

SUNDAY July 21, 2019

What I will do to feel the way I want to feel

TO-DO ... what would be comforting?

1. _____
2. _____
3. _____
_____
_____
_____

ENVISION
What rituals support your Core Desired Feelings?

SOUL PROMPT In terms of my livelihood, my greatest desire is

Let the pain, the joy, the desire soften you.

INVOCATION

MONDAY July 22, 2019 | *Sun enters Leo*

MY CORE DESIRED FEELINGS

What I will do to feel the way I want to feel

SCHEDULE ... joy expands time

: _____
: _____
: _____
: _____
: _____
: _____
: _____
: _____
: _____
: _____
: _____
: _____
: _____
: _____
: _____
: _____
: _____

TO-DO ... keep your soul on the agenda

1. _____
2. _____
3. _____
   _____
   _____
   _____

BODY & WELLNESS My body knows ...

DEVOTION Devotion creates miracles.

NOT WORKING ... does it feel light or heavy?

STOP DOING ... speak up

GRATEFUL ... ask for more

Because ...

ARDENT

Let yourself be found.

TUESDAY July 23, 2019

MY CORE DESIRED FEELINGS *What I will do to feel the way I want to feel*

SCHEDULE ... take up space

: _____
: _____
: _____
: _____
: _____
: _____
: _____
: _____
: _____
: _____
: _____
: _____
: _____
: _____
: _____
: _____

TO-DO ... make choices that liberate you

1. _____
2. _____
3. _____
_____
_____
_____

BODY & WELLNESS I will tend to my body ...

DEVOTION I will contemplate ...

NOT WORKING ... name it so you can change it

STOP DOING ... *No* makes way for *Yes*

GRATEFUL ... gratitude puts everything into perspective   *Because ...*

Question your teachers.

FLEXIBLE

WEDNESDAY July 24, 2019

MY CORE DESIRED FEELINGS　　　　　　　　　　*What I will do to feel the way I want to feel*

SCHEDULE ... what do you really want to happen?　　　**TO-DO** ... imagine

: _____　　1. _____

: _____　　2. _____

: _____　　3. _____

: _____　　_____

: _____　　_____

: _____　　_____

: _____　　**BODY & WELLNESS** I will nourish my body ...

: _____

: _____　　**DEVOTION** I will pray for (who/what) ...

: _____

: _____

: _____　　**NOT WORKING** ... don't hold back

: _____

: _____

: _____　　**STOP DOING** ... clarity is power

: _____

: _____

GRATEFUL ... note WHY you're grateful　　　　*Because ...*

Love is always the right thing to do.

SULTRY

THURSDAY July 25, 2019

MY CORE DESIRED FEELINGS

What I will do to feel the way I want to feel

SCHEDULE ... leave room for magic

: _____
: _____
: _____
: _____
: _____
: _____
: _____
: _____
: _____
: _____
: _____
: _____
: _____
: _____
: _____
: _____

TO-DO ... prioritize pleasure

1. _____
2. _____
3. _____
   _____
   _____
   _____

BODY & WELLNESS My body helps me ...

DEVOTION My meditation will be ...

NOT WORKING ... claim it. Tame it.

STOP DOING ... don't take any crap

GRATEFUL ... be a beacon of optimism

Because ...

A prayer: may my suffering be of service.

LUSH

FRIDAY July 26, 2019

MY CORE DESIRED FEELINGS

What I will do to feel the way I want to feel

SCHEDULE ... work for Love

: _____
: _____
: _____
: _____
: _____
: _____
: _____
: _____
: _____
: _____
: _____
: _____
: _____
: _____
: _____
: _____

TO-DO ... do what lights you up

1. _____
2. _____
3. _____
   _____
   _____

BODY & WELLNESS My body is ...

DEVOTION I will dedicate this day to ...

NOT WORKING ... feel free

STOP DOING ... freedom is your birthright

GRATEFUL ... specificity intensifies gratitude

Because ...

HARMONIOUS

Decide to just get over it. Let it be that simple.

SATURDAY July 27, 2019
Venus enters Leo

MY CORE DESIRED FEELINGS

TO-DO ... relax ... rebel ... rest

1. _____
2. _____
3. _____
   _____
   _____
   _____

REFLECT
Which Core Desired Feeling seems farthest away? How do you feel about that?

SUNDAY July 28, 2019

What I will do to feel the way I want to feel

TO-DO ... visualize your ideal life

1. _____
2. _____
3. _____
   _____
   _____
   _____

ENVISION
What would help you feel your Core Desired Feelings this week?

SOUL PROMPT Three words about my potential

Happiness returns more quickly when you give yourself permission to be blue.

SELF-SUFFICIENT

MONDAY July 29, 2019

MY CORE DESIRED FEELINGS

What I will do to feel the way I want to feel

SCHEDULE ... simplicity is freedom

: _____
: _____
: _____
: _____
: _____
: _____
: _____
: _____
: _____
: _____
: _____
: _____
: _____
: _____
: _____

TO-DO ... believe in yourself

1. _____
2. _____
3. _____
   _____
   _____
   _____

BODY & WELLNESS My body is telling me ...

DEVOTION I will light a candle for ...

NOT WORKING ... does it feel light or heavy?

STOP DOING ... speak up

GRATEFUL ... ask for more

Because ...

PRIMAL JOY

Focus on opening, opening, opening.

TUESDAY July 30, 2019

MY CORE DESIRED FEELINGS   *What I will do to feel the way I want to feel*

SCHEDULE ... does it light you up?

: _____
: _____
: _____
: _____
: _____
: _____
: _____
: _____
: _____
: _____
: _____
: _____
: _____
: _____
: _____
: _____
: _____

TO-DO ... clarity creates simplicity

1. _____
2. _____
3. _____
   _____
   _____
   _____

BODY & WELLNESS I will respect my body ...

DEVOTION I will have faith that ...

NOT WORKING ... name it so you can change it

STOP DOING ... *No* makes way for *Yes*

GRATEFUL ... gratitude puts everything into perspective   *Because* ...

TENACIOUS

Find out how powerful you are.

WEDNESDAY July 31, 2019 | ● *New Moon in Leo | Mercury stations Direct in Cancer*

MY CORE DESIRED FEELINGS *What I will do to feel the way I want to feel*

SCHEDULE ... joy expands time

: _____
: _____
: _____
: _____
: _____
: _____
: _____
: _____
: _____
: _____
: _____
: _____
: _____
: _____
: _____
: _____

TO-DO ... keep your soul on the agenda

1. _____
2. _____
3. _____
  _____
  _____
  _____

BODY & WELLNESS My body knows ...

DEVOTION Devotion creates miracles.

NOT WORKING ... don't hold back

STOP DOING ... clarity is power

GRATEFUL ... note WHY you're grateful   *Because ...*

VIVID

Create where you belong.

IDEAS. DESIRES. WISDOM. ... anything is possible

THE PAST MONTH: Reflect. Clarify. Create.

ROOT DEEPLY TO BE TRULY OPEN.

Stay anchored to your Core Desired Feelings so you can be open to different ways (which may be different than you imagined) that those feelings and experiences can come into your life.

MY CORE DESIRED FEELINGS
My CDFs are strongest in… I feel most aligned with… I'm moving toward…
I want to give more attention to…

MY GOALS & INTENTIONS
My goals are bringing my CDFs to life… I need to change up, refine or deepen…
To move closer to my goals & intentions I…

WHAT'S REALLY WORKING, YA!
I really felt [your CDF] when… This month I was so brilliant…
I created… I felt… I allowed… I accomplished…

WHAT NEEDS TO SHIFT
I felt disappointed… The challenge…

THE NEW MONTH: Envision. Intend. Energize.

YOU ARE THE ONLY ONE YOU NEED PERMISSION FROM.

"You see, I want a lot. Perhaps I want everything."
— Rainer Maria Rilke

HOW I WILL

be stronger… softer… more determined… less uptight… more flexible… less constricted… more open… less accommodating… more accommodating… less worried… more generous… less doubtful… more trusting… less punishing… more pleasure-creating… less fearful… more loving…

TO MOVE TOWARD MY GOALS & INTENTIONS…

AUGUST
2019

AUGUST

MONDAY	TUESDAY	WEDNESDAY
WEEK 31		
5	6	7
WEEK 32		
12	13	14
WEEK 33		
19	20 Venus enters Virgo	21
WEEK 34		
26	27 **Summer Bank Holiday (UK)**	28
WEEK 35		

I feel the bliss in my core. I increase my capacity for more.

Let the rhythm of this move you into your heart. This is great to recite while moving your body.

THURSDAY	FRIDAY	SATURDAY	SUNDAY
1	2	3	4
8	9	10	**Tisha B'Av (Jewish holiday)** **Eid-al-Adha (Islam)** 11 Mercury enters Leo Jupiter stations Direct in Sagittarius Uranus stations Retrograde in Taurus
○ Full Moon in Aquarius 15	16	Mars enters Virgo 17	18
22	Sun enters Virgo 23	24	25
Mercury enters Virgo 29	● New Moon in Virgo 30	31	

AUGUST

THURSDAY August 1, 2019

MY CORE DESIRED FEELINGS

What I will do to feel the way I want to feel

SCHEDULE ... take up space

: _____
: _____
: _____
: _____
: _____
: _____
: _____
: _____
: _____
: _____
: _____
: _____
: _____
: _____
: _____
: _____

TO-DO ... make choices that liberate you

1. _____
2. _____
3. _____
   _____
   _____

BODY & WELLNESS I will tend to my body ...

DEVOTION I will contemplate ...

NOT WORKING ... claim it. Tame it.

STOP DOING ... don't take any crap

GRATEFUL ... be a beacon of optimism

Because ...

OVER-FLOWING

Root into your longing.

FRIDAY August 2, 2019

MY CORE DESIRED FEELINGS   *What I will do to feel the way I want to feel*

SCHEDULE ... what do you really want to happen?

: _____
: _____
: _____
: _____
: _____
: _____
: _____
: _____
: _____
: _____
: _____
: _____
: _____
: _____
: _____
: _____

TO-DO ... imagine

1. _____
2. _____
3. _____
_____
_____
_____

BODY & WELLNESS I will nourish my body ...

DEVOTION I will pray for (who/what) ...

NOT WORKING ... feel free

STOP DOING ... freedom is your birthright

GRATEFUL ... specificity intensifies gratitude   *Because ...*

SOLID

All pain is a cleansing.

SATURDAY August 3, 2019

MY CORE DESIRED FEELINGS

TO-DO ... let it be easy

1. _____
2. _____
3. _____
   _____
   _____

REFLECT
When you are feeling your CDFs, how does that help you be of more service to others?

SUNDAY August 4, 2019

What I will do to feel the way I want to feel

TO-DO ... make space for the light to enter

1. _____
2. _____
3. _____
   _____
   _____

ENVISION
How will you show up in the world as one of your CDFs?

SOUL PROMPT I wish I were more

LIT UP

Rest is productive.

MONDAY August 5, 2019

MY CORE DESIRED FEELINGS

What I will do to feel the way I want to feel

SCHEDULE ... leave room for magic

: _____
: _____
: _____
: _____
: _____
: _____
: _____
: _____
: _____
: _____
: _____
: _____
: _____
: _____
: _____
: _____
: _____

TO-DO ... prioritize pleasure

1. _____
2. _____
3. _____
   _____
   _____
   _____

BODY & WELLNESS My body helps me ...

DEVOTION My meditation will be ...

NOT WORKING ... does it feel light or heavy?

STOP DOING ... speak up

GRATEFUL ... ask for more

Because ...

Gravitate toward happiness.

TENDER

TUESDAY August 6, 2019

MY CORE DESIRED FEELINGS

What I will do to feel the way I want to feel

SCHEDULE ... work for Love

: _____
: _____
: _____
: _____
: _____
: _____
: _____
: _____
: _____
: _____
: _____
: _____
: _____
: _____
: _____

TO-DO ... do what lights you up

1. _____
2. _____
3. _____
   _____
   _____
   _____

BODY & WELLNESS My body is ...

DEVOTION I will dedicate this day to ...

NOT WORKING ... name it so you can change it

STOP DOING ... *No* makes way for *Yes*

GRATEFUL ... gratitude puts everything into perspective

Because ...

CLEAR

Stand your ground, it's sacred.

WEDNESDAY August 7, 2019

MY CORE DESIRED FEELINGS — *What I will do to feel the way I want to feel*

SCHEDULE ... simplicity is freedom

: _____
: _____
: _____
: _____
: _____
: _____
: _____
: _____
: _____
: _____
: _____
: _____
: _____
: _____
: _____
: _____
: _____

TO-DO ... believe in yourself

1. _____
2. _____
3. _____
   _____
   _____
   _____

BODY & WELLNESS My body is telling me ...

DEVOTION I will light a candle for ...

NOT WORKING ... don't hold back

STOP DOING ... clarity is power

GRATEFUL ... note WHY you're grateful — *Because ...*

Romance the future.

AUTHENTIC

THURSDAY August 8, 2019

MY CORE DESIRED FEELINGS

What I will do to feel the way I want to feel

SCHEDULE ... does it light you up?

___ : _____
___ : _____
___ : _____
___ : _____
___ : _____
___ : _____
___ : _____
___ : _____
___ : _____
___ : _____
___ : _____
___ : _____
___ : _____
___ : _____
___ : _____

TO-DO ... clarity creates simplicity

1. _____
2. _____
3. _____
   _____
   _____
   _____

BODY & WELLNESS I will respect my body ...

DEVOTION I will have faith that ...

NOT WORKING ... claim it. Tame it.

STOP DOING ... don't take any crap

GRATEFUL ... be a beacon of optimism

Because ...

PURPOSEFUL

The future you desire deserves your full attention.

FRIDAY August 9, 2019

MY CORE DESIRED FEELINGS

What I will do to feel the way I want to feel

SCHEDULE ... joy expands time

: _____
: _____
: _____
: _____
: _____
: _____
: _____
: _____
: _____
: _____
: _____
: _____
: _____
: _____
: _____
: _____

TO-DO ... keep your soul on the agenda

1. _____
2. _____
3. _____
   _____
   _____
   _____

BODY & WELLNESS My body knows ...

DEVOTION Devotion creates miracles.

NOT WORKING ... feel free

STOP DOING ... freedom is your birthright

GRATEFUL ... specificity intensifies gratitude

Because ...

COMFORTABLE

Desire leads to truth.

SATURDAY August 10, 2019

MY CORE DESIRED FEELINGS

TO-DO ... what would be comforting?

1. _____
2. _____
3. _____
   _____
   _____
   _____

REFLECT
Have a conversation with one of your CDFs, ask it to give you some guidance.

SUNDAY August 11, 2019

Tisha B'Av (Jewish holiday) | Eid-al-Adha (Islam)
Mercury enters Leo | Jupiter stations Direct in Sagittarius
Uranus stations Retrograde in Taurus

What I will do to feel the way I want to feel

TO-DO ... relax ... rebel ... rest

1. _____
2. _____
3. _____
   _____
   _____
   _____

ENVISION
What spaces or places embody your Core Desired Feelings?

SOUL PROMPT I feel confident when

LUMINOUS

It won't always be this way.

MONDAY August 12, 2019

MY CORE DESIRED FEELINGS   *What I will do to feel the way I want to feel*

SCHEDULE ... take up space

: _____
: _____
: _____
: _____
: _____
: _____
: _____
: _____
: _____
: _____
: _____
: _____
: _____
: _____
: _____
: _____
: _____

TO-DO ... make choices that liberate you

1. _____
2. _____
3. _____
_____
_____
_____

BODY & WELLNESS I will tend to my body ...

DEVOTION I will contemplate ...

NOT WORKING ... does it feel light or heavy?

STOP DOING ... speak up

GRATEFUL ... ask for more   *Because ...*

ORGANIZED

Mediocrity isn't benign, or passive, or neutral. It's soul poison.

TUESDAY August 13, 2019

MY CORE DESIRED FEELINGS

What I will do to feel the way I want to feel

SCHEDULE ... what do you really want to happen?

__ : _____
__ : _____
__ : _____
__ : _____
__ : _____
__ : _____
__ : _____
__ : _____
__ : _____
__ : _____
__ : _____
__ : _____
__ : _____
__ : _____
__ : _____

TO-DO ... imagine

1. _____
2. _____
3. _____
_____
_____
_____

BODY & WELLNESS I will nourish my body ...

DEVOTION I will pray for (who/what) ...

NOT WORKING ... name it so you can change it

STOP DOING ... *No* makes way for *Yes*

GRATEFUL ... gratitude puts everything into perspective

Because ...

INDULGENCE

Going without, and holding out, is better than selling out.

WEDNESDAY August 14, 2019

MY CORE DESIRED FEELINGS

What I will do to feel the way I want to feel

SCHEDULE ... leave room for magic

: _____
: _____
: _____
: _____
: _____
: _____
: _____
: _____
: _____
: _____
: _____
: _____
: _____
: _____
: _____
: _____

TO-DO ... prioritize pleasure

1. _____
2. _____
3. _____
_____
_____
_____

BODY & WELLNESS My body helps me ...

DEVOTION My meditation will be ...

NOT WORKING ... don't hold back

STOP DOING ... clarity is power

GRATEFUL ... note WHY you're grateful

Because ...

SOFT

Giving is the antidote to emptiness.

THURSDAY August 15, 2019 | ○ *Full Moon in Aquarius*

MY CORE DESIRED FEELINGS

What I will do to feel the way I want to feel

SCHEDULE ... work for Love

: _____
: _____
: _____
: _____
: _____
: _____
: _____
: _____
: _____
: _____
: _____
: _____
: _____
: _____
: _____
: _____

TO-DO ... do what lights you up

1. _____
2. _____
3. _____
   _____
   _____
   _____

BODY & WELLNESS My body is ...

DEVOTION I will dedicate this day to ...

NOT WORKING ... claim it. Tame it.

STOP DOING ... don't take any crap

GRATEFUL ... be a beacon of optimism

Because ...

ORGASMIC

Your freedom is an urgent matter.

FRIDAY August 16, 2019

MY CORE DESIRED FEELINGS | *What I will do to feel the way I want to feel*

SCHEDULE ... simplicity is freedom

: _____
: _____
: _____
: _____
: _____
: _____
: _____
: _____
: _____
: _____
: _____
: _____
: _____
: _____
: _____
: _____
: _____

TO-DO ... believe in yourself

1. _____
2. _____
3. _____
   _____
   _____
   _____

BODY & WELLNESS My body is telling me ...

DEVOTION I will light a candle for ...

NOT WORKING ... feel free

STOP DOING ... freedom is your birthright

GRATEFUL ... specificity intensifies gratitude | *Because ...*

Believe in an abundant universe

EUPHORIC

SATURDAY August 17, 2019
Mars enters Virgo

MY CORE DESIRED FEELINGS

TO-DO ... visualize your ideal life

1. _____
2. _____
3. _____
_____
_____
_____

REFLECT
Hands on your heart, eyes closed, recite your CDFs and see what images arise.

SUNDAY August 18, 2019

What I will do to feel the way I want to feel

TO-DO ... let it be easy

1. _____
2. _____
3. _____
_____
_____
_____

ENVISION
What Core Desired Feeling(s) need extra attention this week?

SOUL PROMPT The best advice you have ever been given

ENRICHED

Why would you want to delay gratification?

MONDAY August 19, 2019

MY CORE DESIRED FEELINGS   *What I will do to feel the way I want to feel*

SCHEDULE ... does it light you up?

: _____
: _____
: _____
: _____
: _____
: _____
: _____
: _____
: _____
: _____
: _____
: _____
: _____
: _____
: _____
: _____

TO-DO ... clarity creates simplicity

1. _____
2. _____
3. _____
   _____
   _____
   _____

BODY & WELLNESS I will respect my body ...

DEVOTION I will have faith that ...

NOT WORKING ... does it feel light or heavy?

STOP DOING ... speak up

GRATEFUL ... ask for more   *Because ...*

Become a testament to the force of tenderness.

WONDROUS

TUESDAY August 20, 2019

MY CORE DESIRED FEELINGS

What I will do to feel the way I want to feel

SCHEDULE ... joy expands time

: _____
: _____
: _____
: _____
: _____
: _____
: _____
: _____
: _____
: _____
: _____
: _____
: _____
: _____
: _____
: _____

TO-DO ... keep your soul on the agenda

1. _____
2. _____
3. _____
   _____
   _____
   _____

BODY & WELLNESS My body knows ...

DEVOTION Devotion creates miracles.

NOT WORKING ... name it so you can change it

STOP DOING ... *No* makes way for *Yes*

GRATEFUL ... gratitude puts everything into perspective

Because ...

SPIRIT

Motives design our reality.

WEDNESDAY August 21, 2019 | *Venus enters Virgo*

MY CORE DESIRED FEELINGS

What I will do to feel the way I want to feel

SCHEDULE ... take up space

   : _____
   : _____
   : _____
   : _____
   : _____
   : _____
   : _____
   : _____
   : _____
   : _____
   : _____
   : _____
   : _____
   : _____
   : _____

TO-DO ... make choices that liberate you

1. _____
2. _____
3. _____
    _____
    _____
    _____

BODY & WELLNESS I will tend to my body ...

DEVOTION I will contemplate ...

NOT WORKING ... don't hold back

STOP DOING ... clarity is power

GRATEFUL ... note WHY you're grateful

Because ...

UNDERSTOOD

Strong preferences = deliberate creation.

THURSDAY August 22, 2019

MY CORE DESIRED FEELINGS

What I will do to feel the way I want to feel

SCHEDULE ... what do you really want to happen?

: _____
: _____
: _____
: _____
: _____
: _____
: _____
: _____
: _____
: _____
: _____
: _____
: _____
: _____
: _____
: _____

TO-DO ... imagine

1. _____
2. _____
3. _____
   _____
   _____
   _____

BODY & WELLNESS I will nourish my body ...

DEVOTION I will pray for (who/what) ...

NOT WORKING ... claim it. Tame it.

STOP DOING ... don't take any crap

GRATEFUL ... be a beacon of optimism

Because ...

SOUL-SATISFIED

When the Phoenix rises from the flames, she is even more beautiful than before.

FRIDAY August 23, 2019 | *Sun enters Virgo*

MY CORE DESIRED FEELINGS   *What I will do to feel the way I want to feel*

SCHEDULE ... leave room for magic

: _____
: _____
: _____
: _____
: _____
: _____
: _____
: _____
: _____
: _____
: _____
: _____
: _____
: _____
: _____
: _____
: _____

TO-DO ... prioritize pleasure

1. _____
2. _____
3. _____
   _____
   _____
   _____

BODY & WELLNESS My body helps me ...

DEVOTION My meditation will be ...

NOT WORKING ... feel free

STOP DOING ... freedom is your birthright

GRATEFUL ... specificity intensifies gratitude   *Because ...*

Find the comfort in the rhythm of commitment.

PROGRESSIVE

SATURDAY August 24, 2019

MY CORE DESIRED FEELINGS

TO-DO ... make space for the light to enter

1. _____
2. _____
3. _____
   _____
   _____
   _____

REFLECT
The Core Desired Feeling closest to my heart is...

SUNDAY August 25, 2019

What I will do to feel the way I want to feel

TO-DO ... what would be comforting?

1. _____
2. _____
3. _____
   _____
   _____
   _____

ENVISION
How are your Core Desired Feelings experienced in your body?

SOUL PROMPT Two things you are doing to care for your body

OUTRAGEOUS

Your body remembers everything that really matters.

MONDAY August 26, 2019

MY CORE DESIRED FEELINGS   *What I will do to feel the way I want to feel*

SCHEDULE ... work for Love

: _____
: _____
: _____
: _____
: _____
: _____
: _____
: _____
: _____
: _____
: _____
: _____
: _____
: _____
: _____
: _____
: _____

TO-DO ... do what lights you up

1. _____
2. _____
3. _____
_____
_____
_____

BODY & WELLNESS My body is ...

DEVOTION I will dedicate this day to ...

NOT WORKING ... does it feel light or heavy?

STOP DOING ... speak up

GRATEFUL ... ask for more   *Because ...*

ARTICULATE

Look for the Light with more intensity than ever.

TUESDAY August 27, 2019 | *Summer Bank Holiday (UK)*

MY CORE DESIRED FEELINGS   *What I will do to feel the way I want to feel*

SCHEDULE ... simplicity is freedom

: _____
: _____
: _____
: _____
: _____
: _____
: _____
: _____
: _____
: _____
: _____
: _____
: _____
: _____
: _____

TO-DO ... believe in yourself

1. _____
2. _____
3. _____
_____
_____
_____

BODY & WELLNESS My body is telling me ...

DEVOTION I will light a candle for ...

NOT WORKING ... name it so you can change it

STOP DOING ... *No* makes way for *Yes*

GRATEFUL ... gratitude puts everything into perspective   *Because ...*

COMMUNION

Give what you want to get.

WEDNESDAY August 28, 2019

MY CORE DESIRED FEELINGS

What I will do to feel the way I want to feel

SCHEDULE ... does it light you up?

: _____
: _____
: _____
: _____
: _____
: _____
: _____
: _____
: _____
: _____
: _____
: _____
: _____
: _____
: _____
: _____
: _____

TO-DO ... clarity creates simplicity

1. _____
2. _____
3. _____
   _____
   _____
   _____

BODY & WELLNESS I will respect my body ...

DEVOTION I will have faith that ...

NOT WORKING ... don't hold back

STOP DOING ... clarity is power

GRATEFUL ... note WHY you're grateful

Because ...

Sometimes, explaining yourself burns energy you could use for moving on.

IMAGINATIVE

THURSDAY August 29, 2019 | *Mercury enters Virgo*

MY CORE DESIRED FEELINGS   *What I will do to feel the way I want to feel*

SCHEDULE ... joy expands time

: _____
: _____
: _____
: _____
: _____
: _____
: _____
: _____
: _____
: _____
: _____
: _____
: _____
: _____
: _____
: _____

TO-DO ... keep your soul on the agenda

1. _____
2. _____
3. _____
   _____
   _____

BODY & WELLNESS My body knows ...

DEVOTION Devotion creates miracles.

NOT WORKING ... claim it. Tame it.

STOP DOING ... don't take any crap

GRATEFUL ... be a beacon of optimism   *Because ...*

GLAMOROUS

Give it all you got, and then let it go.

FRIDAY August 30, 2019 | ● *New Moon in Virgo*

MY CORE DESIRED FEELINGS

What I will do to feel the way I want to feel

SCHEDULE ... take up space

TO-DO ... make choices that liberate you

1. _____
2. _____
3. _____

BODY & WELLNESS I will tend to my body ...

DEVOTION I will contemplate ...

NOT WORKING ... feel free

STOP DOING ... freedom is your birthright

GRATEFUL ... specificity intensifies gratitude

Because ...

Want what you want with all your heart.

OCEANIC

SATURDAY August 31, 2019

MY CORE DESIRED FEELINGS

What I will do to feel the way I want to feel

TO-DO ... relax ... rebel ... rest

1. _____
2. _____
3. _____
_____
_____
_____

TO-DO ... visualize your ideal life

1. _____
2. _____
3. _____
_____
_____
_____

REFLECT
A prayer: Thank you for the clarity and courage to make choices that favor my Core Desired Feelings.

ENVISION
A prayer: Thank you for guiding me to express and experience my Core Desired Feelings.

SOUL PROMPT I'm feeling tender about

GENEROUS

Thank you for doing what you say you're going to do.

IDEAS. DESIRES. WISDOM. ... keep your heart open

JUBILANT

THE PAST MONTH: Reflect. Clarify. Create.

YOUR HEART IS YOUR HIGHEST INTELLIGENCE.
Everything we do is driven by the desire to feel a certain way. Everything. So clarity of desired feelings = clarity of action.

MY CORE DESIRED FEELINGS
My CDFs are strongest in… I feel most aligned with… I'm moving toward…
I want to give more attention to…

MY GOALS & INTENTIONS
My goals are bringing my CDFs to life… I need to change up, refine or deepen…
To move closer to my goals & intentions I…

WHAT'S REALLY WORKING, YA!
I really felt [your CDF] when… This month I was so brilliant…
I created… I felt… I allowed… I accomplished…

WHAT NEEDS TO SHIFT
I felt disappointed… The challenge…

THE NEW MONTH: Envision. Intend. Energize.

GIVE ALL OF YOURSELF.
"Holding nothing back. The reward for holding nothing back is feeling your place in the universe."
— Mark Nepo

HOW I WILL

be stronger… softer… more determined… less uptight… more flexible… less constricted… more open… less accommodating… more accommodating… less worried… more generous… less doubtful… more trusting… less punishing… more pleasure-creating… less fearful… more loving…

TO MOVE TOWARD MY GOALS & INTENTIONS…

SEPTEMBER
2019

All of life is in my every breath. I have all I need at all times.

Feet on the ground, left hand on heart, right hand on belly. Take a deep breath in between each repetition.

MONDAY	TUESDAY	WEDNESDAY
WEEK 35		
Labor/Labour Day **Ganesh Chaturthi begins (Hindu)** 2 — **WEEK 36**	3	4
9 — **WEEK 37**	**Ashura (Islam)** 10	11
16 — **WEEK 38**	17	Saturn stations Direct in Capricorn 18
Autumn Equinox/ Mabon (Pagan) Sun enters Libra 23 — **WEEK 39**	24	25
30 — **WEEK 40**		

THURSDAY	FRIDAY	SATURDAY	SUNDAY
			Father's Day (AUS) 1 **Ra's as-Sanah (Islam)**
5	6	7	8
Ganesh Chaturthi 12 **ends (Hindu)**	○ Full Moon in Pisces 13	Mercury enters Libra 14 Venus enters Libra	15
19	20	21	22
26	27	● New Moon in Libra 28	**Rosh Hashanah** 29 **begins - evening** **(Jewish holiday)** **Navratri begins (Hindu)**

SEPTEMBER

SUNDAY September 1, 2019 | *Father's Day (AUS) | Ra's as-Sanah (Islam)*

MY CORE DESIRED FEELINGS   *What I will do to feel the way I want to feel*

TO-DO

1. _____
2. _____
3. _____
_____
_____
_____

TO-DO

1. _____
2. _____
3. _____
_____
_____
_____

REFLECT
What Core Desired Feeling felt most alive in your life? Why/how?

ENVISION
What rituals support your Core Desired Feelings?

SOUL PROMPT I'm feeling tender about

SOULFUL

Thank you for doing what you say you're going to do.

MONDAY September 2, 2019 | *Labor/Labour Day | Ganesh Chaturthi begins (Hindu)*

MY CORE DESIRED FEELINGS *What I will do to feel the way I want to feel*

SCHEDULE ... what do you really want to happen? **TO-DO** ... imagine

: _____ 1. _____

: _____ 2. _____

: _____ 3. _____

: _____

: _____

: _____

: _____ **BODY & WELLNESS** I will nourish my body ...

: _____

: _____ **DEVOTION** I will pray for (who/what) ...

: _____

: _____ **NOT WORKING** ... does it feel light or heavy?

: _____

: _____ **STOP DOING** ... speak up

: _____

: _____

GRATEFUL ... ask for more *Because ...*

PRESENCE

Discernment is our wisdom coming alive.

TUESDAY September 3, 2019

MY CORE DESIRED FEELINGS

What I will do to feel the way I want to feel

SCHEDULE ... leave room for magic

: _____
: _____
: _____
: _____
: _____
: _____
: _____
: _____
: _____
: _____
: _____
: _____
: _____
: _____
: _____
: _____

TO-DO ... prioritize pleasure

1. _____
2. _____
3. _____
   _____
   _____
   _____

BODY & WELLNESS My body helps me ...

DEVOTION My meditation will be ...

NOT WORKING ... name it so you can change it

STOP DOING ... *No* makes way for *Yes*

GRATEFUL ... gratitude puts everything into perspective

Because ...

AT HOME

Feel the doubt, serve anyway.

WEDNESDAY September 4, 2019

MY CORE DESIRED FEELINGS

What I will do to feel the way I want to feel

SCHEDULE ... work for Love

: _____
: _____
: _____
: _____
: _____
: _____
: _____
: _____
: _____
: _____
: _____
: _____
: _____
: _____
: _____
: _____

TO-DO ... do what lights you up

1. _____
2. _____
3. _____
_____
_____
_____

BODY & WELLNESS My body is ...

DEVOTION I will dedicate this day to ...

NOT WORKING ... don't hold back

STOP DOING ... clarity is power

GRATEFUL ... note WHY you're grateful

Because ...

TOGETHER

Aim for the heart, that's where the courage is.

THURSDAY September 5, 2019

MY CORE DESIRED FEELINGS

What I will do to feel the way I want to feel

SCHEDULE ... simplicity is freedom

: _____
: _____
: _____
: _____
: _____
: _____
: _____
: _____
: _____
: _____
: _____
: _____
: _____
: _____

TO-DO ... believe in yourself

1. _____
2. _____
3. _____
   _____
   _____

BODY & WELLNESS My body is telling me ...

DEVOTION I will light a candle for ...

NOT WORKING ... claim it. Tame it.

STOP DOING ... don't take any crap

GRATEFUL ... be a beacon of optimism

Because ...

CHERISH

Words energize.

FRIDAY September 6, 2019

MY CORE DESIRED FEELINGS — *What I will do to feel the way I want to feel*

SCHEDULE ... does it light you up?

: _____
: _____
: _____
: _____
: _____
: _____
: _____
: _____
: _____
: _____
: _____
: _____
: _____
: _____
: _____
: _____

TO-DO ... clarity creates simplicity

1. _____
2. _____
3. _____
_____
_____
_____

BODY & WELLNESS I will respect my body ...

DEVOTION I will have faith that ...

NOT WORKING ... feel free

STOP DOING ... freedom is your birthright

GRATEFUL ... specificity intensifies gratitude

Because ...

FULLY EXPRESSED

Make a new vow.

SATURDAY September 7, 2019

MY CORE DESIRED FEELINGS

TO-DO ... let it be easy

1. _____
2. _____
3. _____
_____
_____
_____

REFLECT
Which Core Desired Feeling seems farthest away? How do you feel about that?

SUNDAY September 8, 2019

What I will do to feel the way I want to feel

TO-DO ... make space for the light to enter

1. _____
2. _____
3. _____
_____
_____
_____

ENVISION
What would help you feel your Core Desired Feelings this week?

SOUL PROMPT I aim to

PROSPEROUS

You become what you worship.

MONDAY September 9, 2019

MY CORE DESIRED FEELINGS   *What I will do to feel the way I want to feel*

SCHEDULE ... joy expands time

_:_ _____
_:_ _____
_:_ _____
_:_ _____
_:_ _____
_:_ _____
_:_ _____
_:_ _____
_:_ _____
_:_ _____
_:_ _____
_:_ _____
_:_ _____
_:_ _____
_:_ _____
_:_ _____
_:_ _____

TO-DO ... keep your soul on the agenda

1. _____
2. _____
3. _____
_____
_____
_____

BODY & WELLNESS My body knows ...

DEVOTION Devotion creates miracles.

NOT WORKING ... does it feel light or heavy?

STOP DOING ... speak up

GRATEFUL ... ask for more   *Because ...*

Your creativity is your salvation.

ALLURING

TUESDAY September 10, 2019 | *Ashura (Islam)*

MY CORE DESIRED FEELINGS

What I will do to feel the way I want to feel

SCHEDULE ... does it light you up?

: _____
: _____
: _____
: _____
: _____
: _____
: _____
: _____
: _____
: _____
: _____
: _____
: _____
: _____
: _____
: _____

TO-DO ... make choices that liberate you

1. _____
2. _____
3. _____
   _____
   _____
   _____

BODY & WELLNESS I will tend to my body ...

DEVOTION I will contemplate ...

NOT WORKING ... name it so you can change it

STOP DOING ... *No* makes way for *Yes*

GRATEFUL ... gratitude puts everything into perspective   *Because ...*

GRATEFUL

Your soul is rooting for you.

WEDNESDAY September 11, 2019

MY CORE DESIRED FEELINGS   *What I will do to feel the way I want to feel*

SCHEDULE ... let it be easy

: _____
: _____
: _____
: _____
: _____
: _____
: _____
: _____
: _____
: _____
: _____
: _____
: _____
: _____
: _____
: _____
: _____

TO-DO ... imagine

1. _____
2. _____
3. _____
   _____
   _____
   _____

BODY & WELLNESS I will nourish my body ...

DEVOTION I will pray for (who/what) ...

NOT WORKING ... don't hold back

STOP DOING ... clarity is power

GRATEFUL ... note WHY you're grateful   *Because ...*

You're going to get off course. That's part of the journey. Just come back to it.

WHIMSICAL

THURSDAY September 12, 2019 | *Ganesh Chaturthi ends (Hindu)*

MY CORE DESIRED FEELINGS   *What I will do to feel the way I want to feel*

SCHEDULE ... take up space

: _____
: _____
: _____
: _____
: _____
: _____
: _____
: _____
: _____
: _____
: _____
: _____
: _____
: _____
: _____
: _____

TO-DO ... prioritize pleasure

1. _____
2. _____
3. _____
   _____
   _____
   _____

BODY & WELLNESS My body helps me ...

DEVOTION My meditation will be ...

NOT WORKING ... claim it. Tame it.

STOP DOING ... don't take any crap

GRATEFUL ... be a beacon of optimism   *Because ...*

ALIGNED

Move the way your soul likes to move.

FRIDAY September 13, 2019 | ○ *Full Moon in Pisces*

MY CORE DESIRED FEELINGS

What I will do to feel the way I want to feel

SCHEDULE ... what do you really want to happen?

: _____
: _____
: _____
: _____
: _____
: _____
: _____
: _____
: _____
: _____
: _____
: _____
: _____
: _____
: _____
: _____
: _____

TO-DO ... do what lights you up

1. _____
2. _____
3. _____
   _____
   _____
   _____

BODY & WELLNESS My body is ...

DEVOTION I will dedicate this day to ...

NOT WORKING ... feel free

STOP DOING ... freedom is your birthright

GRATEFUL ... specificity intensifies gratitude

Because ...

Happiness is carbonated consciousness.

SELF-NURTURED

SATURDAY September 14, 2019

Mercury enters Libra | Venus enters Libra

MY CORE DESIRED FEELINGS

SUNDAY September 15, 2019

What I will do to feel the way I want to feel

TO-DO ... what would be comforting?

1. _____
2. _____
3. _____
_____
_____
_____

TO-DO ... relax ... rebel ... rest

1. _____
2. _____
3. _____
_____
_____
_____

REFLECT
When you are feeling your CDFs, how does that help you be of more service to others?

ENVISION
How will you show up in the world as one of your CDFs?

SOUL PROMPT One word to describe my current struggle

KICK-ASS

Greet your pain. It brings gifts.

MONDAY September 16, 2019

MY CORE DESIRED FEELINGS   *What I will do to feel the way I want to feel*

SCHEDULE ... leave room for magic

: _____
: _____
: _____
: _____
: _____
: _____
: _____
: _____
: _____
: _____
: _____
: _____
: _____
: _____
: _____
: _____

TO-DO ... believe in yourself

1. _____
2. _____
3. _____
   _____
   _____
   _____

BODY & WELLNESS My body is telling me ...

DEVOTION I will light a candle for ...

NOT WORKING ... does it feel light or heavy?

STOP DOING ... speak up

GRATEFUL ... ask for more   *Because ...*

Choose the joy.

SAFE

TUESDAY September 17, 2019

MY CORE DESIRED FEELINGS

What I will do to feel the way I want to feel

SCHEDULE ... work for Love

: _____
: _____
: _____
: _____
: _____
: _____
: _____
: _____
: _____
: _____
: _____
: _____
: _____
: _____
: _____
: _____
: _____

TO-DO ... clarity creates simplicity

1. _____
2. _____
3. _____
   _____
   _____
   _____

BODY & WELLNESS I will respect my body ...

DEVOTION I will have faith that ...

NOT WORKING ... name it so you can change it

STOP DOING ... *No* makes way for *Yes*

GRATEFUL ... gratitude puts everything into perspective

Because ...

CHILDLIKE

Tell people what you're doing that's working.

WEDNESDAY September 18, 2019 | *Saturn stations Direct in Capricorn*

MY CORE DESIRED FEELINGS   *What I will do to feel the way I want to feel*

SCHEDULE ... simplicity is freedom

: _____
: _____
: _____
: _____
: _____
: _____
: _____
: _____
: _____
: _____
: _____
: _____
: _____
: _____
: _____
: _____
: _____

TO-DO ... keep your soul on the agenda

1. _____
2. _____
3. _____
_____
_____
_____

BODY & WELLNESS My body knows ...

DEVOTION Devotion creates miracles.

NOT WORKING ... don't hold back

STOP DOING ... clarity is power

GRATEFUL ... note WHY you're grateful   *Because ...*

you are worthy of your desires

OVER-JOYED

THURSDAY September 19, 2019

MY CORE DESIRED FEELINGS

What I will do to feel the way I want to feel

SCHEDULE ... take up space

: _____
: _____
: _____
: _____
: _____
: _____
: _____
: _____
: _____
: _____
: _____
: _____
: _____
: _____
: _____

TO-DO ... make choices that liberate you

1. _____
2. _____
3. _____
   _____
   _____
   _____

BODY & WELLNESS I will tend to my body ...

DEVOTION I will contemplate ...

NOT WORKING ... claim it. Tame it.

STOP DOING ... don't take any crap

GRATEFUL ... be a beacon of optimism

Because ...

Stay close to what matters most.

GENUINE

FRIDAY September 20, 2019

MY CORE DESIRED FEELINGS   *What I will do to feel the way I want to feel*

SCHEDULE ... work for Love

: _____
: _____
: _____
: _____
: _____
: _____
: _____
: _____
: _____
: _____
: _____
: _____
: _____
: _____
: _____
: _____
: _____

TO-DO ... imagine

1. _____
2. _____
3. _____
   _____
   _____
   _____

BODY & WELLNESS I will nourish my body ...

DEVOTION I will pray for (who/what) ...

NOT WORKING ... feel free

STOP DOING ... freedom is your birthright

GRATEFUL ... specificity intensifies gratitude   *Because ...*

Decide for yourself.

PASSION

SATURDAY September 21, 2019

MY CORE DESIRED FEELINGS

TO-DO ... visualize your ideal life

1. _____
2. _____
3. _____
   _____
   _____
   _____

REFLECT
Have a conversation with one of your CDFs, ask it to give you some guidance.

SOUL PROMPT I'm growing

ELATED

SUNDAY September 22, 2019

What I will do to feel the way I want to feel

TO-DO ... let it be easy

1. _____
2. _____
3. _____
   _____
   _____
   _____

ENVISION
What spaces or places embody your Core Desired Feelings?

The job isn't done until you say "thank you".

MONDAY September 23, 2019 | *Autumn Equinox/Mabon | Sun enters Libra*

MY CORE DESIRED FEELINGS   *What I will do to feel the way I want to feel*

SCHEDULE ... does it light you up?   **TO-DO** ... prioritize pleasure

: _____   1. _____
: _____   2. _____
: _____   3. _____
: _____   _____
: _____   _____
: _____   _____
: _____
: _____   **BODY & WELLNESS** My body helps me ...
: _____
: _____
: _____   **DEVOTION** My meditation will be ...
: _____
: _____
: _____   **NOT WORKING** ... does it feel light or heavy?
: _____
: _____
: _____   **STOP DOING** ... speak up
: _____
: _____

GRATEFUL ... ask for more   *Because ...*

Fall madly in love with your humanity.

ENRAPTURED

TUESDAY September 24, 2019

MY CORE DESIRED FEELINGS

What I will do to feel the way I want to feel

SCHEDULE ... joy expands time

: _____
: _____
: _____
: _____
: _____
: _____
: _____
: _____
: _____
: _____
: _____
: _____
: _____
: _____
: _____
: _____
: _____

TO-DO ... do what lights you up

1. _____
2. _____
3. _____
   _____
   _____
   _____

BODY & WELLNESS My body is ...

DEVOTION I will dedicate this day to ...

NOT WORKING ... name it so you can change it

STOP DOING ... *No* makes way for *Yes*

GRATEFUL ... gratitude puts everything into perspective

Because ...

LIBERATED

Breathe life into your desires.

WEDNESDAY September 25, 2019

MY CORE DESIRED FEELINGS

What I will do to feel the way I want to feel

SCHEDULE ... take up space

: _____
: _____
: _____
: _____
: _____
: _____
: _____
: _____
: _____
: _____
: _____
: _____
: _____
: _____
: _____
: _____
: _____

TO-DO ... believe in yourself

1. _____
2. _____
3. _____
_____
_____
_____

BODY & WELLNESS My body is telling me ...

DEVOTION I will light a candle for ...

NOT WORKING ... don't hold back

STOP DOING ... clarity is power

GRATEFUL ... note WHY you're grateful

Because ...

The spiritual response to suffering is to befriend it.

POETIC

THURSDAY September 26, 2019

MY CORE DESIRED FEELINGS

What I will do to feel the way I want to feel

SCHEDULE ... what do you really want to happen?

: _____
: _____
: _____
: _____
: _____
: _____
: _____
: _____
: _____
: _____
: _____
: _____
: _____
: _____
: _____

TO-DO ... clarity creates simplicity

1. _____
2. _____
3. _____
   _____
   _____
   _____

BODY & WELLNESS I will respect my body ...

DEVOTION I will have faith that ...

NOT WORKING ... claim it. Tame it.

STOP DOING ... don't take any crap

GRATEFUL ... be a beacon of optimism

Because ...

FULFILLED

Notice how you feel.

FRIDAY September 27, 2019

MY CORE DESIRED FEELINGS   *What I will do to feel the way I want to feel*

SCHEDULE ... leave room for magic

: _____
: _____
: _____
: _____
: _____
: _____
: _____
: _____
: _____
: _____
: _____
: _____
: _____
: _____
: _____

TO-DO ... keep your soul on the agenda

1. _____
2. _____
3. _____
   _____
   _____
   _____

BODY & WELLNESS My body knows ...

DEVOTION Devotion creates miracles.

NOT WORKING ... feel free

STOP DOING ... freedom is your birthright

GRATEFUL ... specificity intensifies gratitude   *Because ...*

Risk being misunderstood. It's usually worth it.

INSIGHTFUL

SATURDAY September 28, 2019
● *New Moon in Libra*

MY CORE DESIRED FEELINGS
_____

TO-DO ... make space for the light to enter

1. _____
2. _____
3. _____
   _____
   _____
   _____

REFLECT
Hands on your heart, eyes closed, recite your CDFs and see what images arise.

SUNDAY September 29, 2019
Navratri begins (Hindu)
Rosh Hashanah begins - evening (Jewish holiday)
_____

What I will do to feel the way I want to feel

TO-DO ... what would be comforting?

1. _____
2. _____
3. _____
   _____
   _____
   _____

ENVISION
What Core Desired Feeling(s) need extra attention this week?

_____

SOUL PROMPT I'm at peace with

FREE. SPIRITED

Collide with your dreams.

MONDAY September 30, 2019

MY CORE DESIRED FEELINGS

What I will do to feel the way I want to feel

SCHEDULE ... work for Love

   : _____
   : _____
   : _____
   : _____
   : _____
   : _____
   : _____
   : _____
   : _____
   : _____
   : _____
   : _____
   : _____
   : _____
   : _____
   : _____

TO-DO ... make choices that liberate you

1. _____
2. _____
3. _____
   _____
   _____
   _____

BODY & WELLNESS I will tend to my body ...

DEVOTION I will contemplate ...

NOT WORKING ... does it feel light or heavy?

STOP DOING ... speak up

GRATEFUL ... ask for more

Because ...

Start where you are and Love what you can.

EXPLORER

THE PAST MONTH: Reflect. Clarify. Create.

MAKE IT THE WAY YOU WANT—TODAY.
When you are clear on how you most want to feel, the pursuit of those feelings—your goals—becomes more satisfying. "Success" really is about the journey.

MY CORE DESIRED FEELINGS
My CDFs are strongest in… I feel most aligned with… I'm moving toward…
I want to give more attention to…

MY GOALS & INTENTIONS
My goals are bringing my CDFs to life… I need to change up, refine or deepen…
To move closer to my goals & intentions I…

WHAT'S REALLY WORKING, YA!
I really felt [your CDF] when… This month I was so brilliant…
I created… I felt… I allowed… I accomplished…

WHAT NEEDS TO SHIFT
I felt disappointed… The challenge…

THE NEW MONTH: Envision. Intend. Energize.

RAISE YOUR STANDARDS.

"Surely everyone realizes, at some point along the way, that he is capable of living a far better life than the one he has chosen."
— Henry Miller, *Big Sur and the Oranges of Hieronymus Bosch*

HOW I WILL
be stronger… softer… more determined… less uptight… more flexible… less constricted… more open… less accommodating… more accommodating… less worried… more generous… less doubtful… more trusting… less punishing… more pleasure-creating… less fearful… more loving…

TO MOVE TOWARD MY GOALS & INTENTIONS…

OCTOBER
2019

Pure.
Innocence.
Safely Held.
Valuable.
Nurtured.
Accepted.
Embraced.
Loved.

These are the words of power from the Love + Radiance Meditation. Silently, out loud, or as a chant, say each word with your most Sacred Intention, your whole heart, feeling each word deeply, on a cellular level.

OCTOBER

	MONDAY	TUESDAY	WEDNESDAY
		Rosh Hashanah ends - evening (Jewish holiday) 1	Pluto stations Direct in Capricorn 2
WEEK 40			
	Navratri ends (Hindu) Labour Day (AUS) 7	**Yom Kippur begins - evening (Jewish holiday)** 8 Venus enters Scorpio	**Yom Kippur ends - evening (Jewish holiday)** 9
WEEK 41			
	Columbus Day (US) Thanksgiving Day (CAN) 14	15	16
WEEK 42			
	Shemini Atzeret (Jewish holiday) 21	**Simchat Torah (Jewish holiday)** 22	Sun enters Scorpio 23
WEEK 43			
	28	29	30
WEEK 44			

THURSDAY	FRIDAY	SATURDAY	SUNDAY
3 Mercury enters Scorpio Mars enters Libra	**4**	**5**	**6** **Daylight Saving Time begins (AUS)**
10	**11**	**12**	**13** **Sukkot begins** ○ Full Moon in Aries
17	**18**	**19**	**20** **Sukkot ends**
24	**25**	**26**	**27** **Diwali (Hindu)** ● New Moon in Scorpio
31 **Halloween/Samhain (Pagan)** Mercury stations Retrograde in Scorpio			

OCTOBER

TUESDAY October 1, 2019 | *Rosh Hashanah ends - evening (Jewish holiday)*

MY CORE DESIRED FEELINGS

What I will do to feel the way I want to feel

SCHEDULE ... simplicity is freedom

TO-DO ... imagine

1. _____
2. _____
3. _____

BODY & WELLNESS I will nourish my body ...

DEVOTION I will pray for (who/what) ...

NOT WORKING ... name it so you can change it

STOP DOING ... *No* makes way for *Yes*

GRATEFUL ... gratitude puts everything into perspective

Because ...

RELEASED

Your Truth is your medicine.

WEDNESDAY October 2, 2019 | *Pluto stations Direct in Capricorn*

MY CORE DESIRED FEELINGS   *What I will do to feel the way I want to feel*

SCHEDULE ... does it light you up?

___ : _____
___ : _____
___ : _____
___ : _____
___ : _____
___ : _____
___ : _____
___ : _____
___ : _____
___ : _____
___ : _____
___ : _____
___ : _____
___ : _____
___ : _____
___ : _____

TO-DO ... prioritize pleasure

1. _____
2. _____
3. _____
_____
_____
_____

BODY & WELLNESS My body helps me ...

DEVOTION My meditation will be ...

NOT WORKING ... don't hold back

STOP DOING ... clarity is power

GRATEFUL ... note WHY you're grateful   *Because ...*

It won't be long now.

ATTUNED

THURSDAY October 3, 2019 | *Mercury enters Scorpio | Mars enters Libra*

MY CORE DESIRED FEELINGS

What I will do to feel the way I want to feel

SCHEDULE ... joy expands time

: _____
: _____
: _____
: _____
: _____
: _____
: _____
: _____
: _____
: _____
: _____
: _____
: _____
: _____
: _____
: _____

TO-DO ... do what lights you up

1. _____
2. _____
3. _____
   _____
   _____
   _____

BODY & WELLNESS My body is ...

DEVOTION I will dedicate this day to ...

NOT WORKING ... claim it. Tame it.

STOP DOING ... don't take any crap

GRATEFUL ... be a beacon of optimism

Because ...

PATIENT

Vividly envision how you want to feel.

FRIDAY October 4, 2019

MY CORE DESIRED FEELINGS *What I will do to feel the way I want to feel*

SCHEDULE ... take up space

: _____
: _____
: _____
: _____
: _____
: _____
: _____
: _____
: _____
: _____
: _____
: _____
: _____
: _____
: _____
: _____

TO-DO ... believe in yourself

1. _____
2. _____
3. _____
   _____
   _____
   _____

BODY & WELLNESS My body is telling me ...

DEVOTION I will light a candle for ...

NOT WORKING ... feel free

STOP DOING ... freedom is your birthright

GRATEFUL ... specificity intensifies gratitude   *Because ...*

Spoiler alert: Love wins.

INCREDIBLE

SATURDAY October 5, 2019

MY CORE DESIRED FEELINGS

TO-DO ... relax ... rebel ... rest

1. _____
2. _____
3. _____
   _____
   _____
   _____

REFLECT
The Core Desired Feeling closest to my heart is...

SOUL PROMPT I rely on

FABULOUS

SUNDAY October 6, 2019
Daylight Saving Time begins (AUS)

What I will do to feel the way I want to feel

TO-DO ... visualize your ideal life

1. _____
2. _____
3. _____
   _____
   _____
   _____

ENVISION
How are your Core Desired Feelings experienced in your body?

Curiosity will save your soul.

MONDAY October 7, 2019 | *Navratri ends (Hindu) | Labour Day (AUS)*

MY CORE DESIRED FEELINGS *What I will do to feel the way I want to feel*

SCHEDULE ... what do you really want to happen?

: _____
: _____
: _____
: _____
: _____
: _____
: _____
: _____
: _____
: _____
: _____
: _____
: _____
: _____
: _____
: _____

TO-DO ... clarity creates simplicity

1. _____
2. _____
3. _____
_____
_____
_____

BODY & WELLNESS I will respect my body ...

DEVOTION I will have faith that ...

NOT WORKING ... does it feel light or heavy?

STOP DOING ... speak up

GRATEFUL ... ask for more   *Because ...*

Sometimes we forget to look at what we're holding on to. Take a look.

LOVING

TUESDAY October 8, 2019 | *Yom Kippur begins - evening (Jewish holiday)* | *Venus enters Scorpio*

MY CORE DESIRED FEELINGS

What I will do to feel the way I want to feel

SCHEDULE ... leave room for magic

   : _____
   : _____
   : _____
   : _____
   : _____
   : _____
   : _____
   : _____
   : _____
   : _____
   : _____
   : _____
   : _____
   : _____
   : _____
   : _____

TO-DO ... keep your soul on the agenda

1. _____
2. _____
3. _____
    _____
    _____
    _____

BODY & WELLNESS My body knows ...

DEVOTION Devotion creates miracles.

NOT WORKING ... name it so you can change it

STOP DOING ... *No* makes way for *Yes*

GRATEFUL ... gratitude puts everything into perspective

Because ...

PROFOUND

Give.

WEDNESDAY October 9, 2019 | *Yom Kippur ends - evening (Jewish holiday)*

MY CORE DESIRED FEELINGS   *What I will do to feel the way I want to feel*

SCHEDULE ... work for Love

: _____
: _____
: _____
: _____
: _____
: _____
: _____
: _____
: _____
: _____
: _____
: _____
: _____
: _____
: _____
: _____

TO-DO ... make choices that liberate you

1. _____
2. _____
3. _____
   _____
   _____
   _____

BODY & WELLNESS I will tend to my body ...

DEVOTION I will contemplate ...

NOT WORKING ... don't hold back

STOP DOING ... clarity is power

GRATEFUL ... note WHY you're grateful   *Because ...*

Let your heart break open.

ORIGINAL

THURSDAY October 10, 2019

MY CORE DESIRED FEELINGS

What I will do to feel the way I want to feel

SCHEDULE ... simplicity is freedom

: _____
: _____
: _____
: _____
: _____
: _____
: _____
: _____
: _____
: _____
: _____
: _____
: _____
: _____
: _____
: _____

TO-DO ... imagine

1. _____
2. _____
3. _____
   _____
   _____
   _____

BODY & WELLNESS I will nourish my body ...

DEVOTION I will pray for (who/what) ...

NOT WORKING ... claim it. Tame it.

STOP DOING ... don't take any crap

GRATEFUL ... be a beacon of optimism

Because ...

LOVELY

find your tribe. love them hard.

FRIDAY October 11, 2019

MY CORE DESIRED FEELINGS   *What I will do to feel the way I want to feel*

SCHEDULE ... does it light you up?

: _____
: _____
: _____
: _____
: _____
: _____
: _____
: _____
: _____
: _____
: _____
: _____
: _____
: _____
: _____
: _____

TO-DO ... prioritize pleasure

1. _____
2. _____
3. _____
   _____
   _____
   _____

BODY & WELLNESS My body helps me ...

DEVOTION My meditation will be ...

NOT WORKING ... feel free

STOP DOING ... freedom is your birthright

GRATEFUL ... specificity intensifies gratitude   *Because ...*

FLAMBOYANT

You must have a relationship with death to live more fully.

SATURDAY October 12, 2019

MY CORE DESIRED FEELINGS

TO-DO ... let it be easy

1. _____
2. _____
3. _____
   _____
   _____
   _____

REFLECT
A prayer: Thank you for the clarity and courage to make choices that favor my Core Desired Feelings.

SUNDAY October 13, 2019
Sukkot begins | ○ Full Moon in Aries

What I will do to feel the way I want to feel

TO-DO ... make space for the light to enter

1. _____
2. _____
3. _____
   _____
   _____
   _____

ENVISION
A prayer: Thank you for guiding me to express and experience my Core Desired Feelings.

SOUL PROMPT I've forgotten how

VITAL

The universe will configure around your best efforts.

MONDAY October 14, 2019 | *Columbus Day (US) | Thanksgiving Day (CAN)*

MY CORE DESIRED FEELINGS   *What I will do to feel the way I want to feel*

SCHEDULE ... joy expands time

: _____
: _____
: _____
: _____
: _____
: _____
: _____
: _____
: _____
: _____
: _____
: _____
: _____
: _____
: _____
: _____

TO-DO ... do what lights you up

1. _____
2. _____
3. _____
   _____
   _____
   _____

BODY & WELLNESS My body is ...

DEVOTION I will dedicate this day to ...

NOT WORKING ... does it feel light or heavy?

STOP DOING ... speak up

GRATEFUL ... ask for more   *Because ...*

Hang out with people who love you.

BLAZING

TUESDAY October 15, 2019

MY CORE DESIRED FEELINGS

What I will do to feel the way I want to feel

SCHEDULE ... take up space

: _____
: _____
: _____
: _____
: _____
: _____
: _____
: _____
: _____
: _____
: _____
: _____
: _____
: _____
: _____

TO-DO ... believe in yourself

1. _____
2. _____
3. _____
   _____
   _____
   _____

BODY & WELLNESS My body is telling me ...

DEVOTION I will light a candle for ...

NOT WORKING ... name it so you can change it

STOP DOING ... *No* makes way for *Yes*

GRATEFUL ... gratitude puts everything into perspective

Because ...

READY

Befriend your loneliness.

WEDNESDAY October 16, 2019

MY CORE DESIRED FEELINGS

What I will do to feel the way I want to feel

SCHEDULE ... what do you really want to happen?

: _____
: _____
: _____
: _____
: _____
: _____
: _____
: _____
: _____
: _____
: _____
: _____
: _____
: _____
: _____
: _____
: _____

TO-DO ... clarity creates simplicity

1. _____
2. _____
3. _____
_____
_____
_____

BODY & WELLNESS I will respect my body ...

DEVOTION I will have faith that ...

NOT WORKING ... don't hold back

STOP DOING ... clarity is power

GRATEFUL ... note WHY you're grateful

Because ...

FIRE-CRACKER

If it doesn't feel good, STOP.

THURSDAY October 17, 2019

MY CORE DESIRED FEELINGS

What I will do to feel the way I want to feel

SCHEDULE ... leave room for magic

: _____
: _____
: _____
: _____
: _____
: _____
: _____
: _____
: _____
: _____
: _____
: _____
: _____
: _____
: _____
: _____
: _____

TO-DO ... keep your soul on the agenda

1. _____
2. _____
3. _____
   _____
   _____
   _____

BODY & WELLNESS My body knows ...

DEVOTION Devotion creates miracles.

NOT WORKING ... claim it. Tame it.

STOP DOING ... don't take any crap

GRATEFUL ... be a beacon of optimism

Because ...

ADVENTUROUS

Compassion is a strategy.

FRIDAY October 18, 2019

MY CORE DESIRED FEELINGS   *What I will do to feel the way I want to feel*

SCHEDULE ... work for Love

: _____
: _____
: _____
: _____
: _____
: _____
: _____
: _____
: _____
: _____
: _____
: _____
: _____
: _____
: _____
: _____

TO-DO ... make choices that liberate you

1. _____
2. _____
3. _____
   _____
   _____
   _____

BODY & WELLNESS I will tend to my body ...

DEVOTION I will contemplate ...

NOT WORKING ... feel free

STOP DOING ... freedom is your birthright

GRATEFUL ... specificity intensifies gratitude   *Because ...*

Destroy before you create. So scary. So effective.

IGNITED

SATURDAY October 19, 2019

MY CORE DESIRED FEELINGS

TO-DO ... what would be comforting?

1. _____
2. _____
3. _____

_____
_____
_____

REFLECT
What Core Desired Feeling felt most alive in your life? Why/how?

SUNDAY October 20, 2019
Sukkot ends

What I will do to feel the way I want to feel

TO-DO ... relax ... rebel ... rest

1. _____
2. _____
3. _____

_____
_____
_____

ENVISION
What rituals support your Core Desired Feelings?

SOUL PROMPT Most favorite recent insight

LIMITLESS

Fantasize.

MONDAY October 21, 2019 | *Shemini Atzeret (Jewish holiday)*

MY CORE DESIRED FEELINGS   *What I will do to feel the way I want to feel*

SCHEDULE ... simplicity is freedom

: _____
: _____
: _____
: _____
: _____
: _____
: _____
: _____
: _____
: _____
: _____
: _____
: _____
: _____
: _____
: _____
: _____

TO-DO ... imagine

1. _____
2. _____
3. _____
   _____
   _____
   _____

BODY & WELLNESS I will nourish my body ...

DEVOTION I will pray for (who/what) ...

NOT WORKING ... does it feel light or heavy?

STOP DOING ... speak up

GRATEFUL ... ask for more   *Because ...*

Your heart...your heart...your heart is where it's at.

FEARLESS

TUESDAY October 22, 2019 | *Simchat Torah (Jewish holiday)*

MY CORE DESIRED FEELINGS

What I will do to feel the way I want to feel

SCHEDULE ... does it light you up?

: _____
: _____
: _____
: _____
: _____
: _____
: _____
: _____
: _____
: _____
: _____
: _____
: _____
: _____
: _____

TO-DO ... *prioritize pleasure*

1. _____
2. _____
3. _____
   _____
   _____
   _____

BODY & WELLNESS My body helps me ...

DEVOTION My meditation will be ...

NOT WORKING ... name it so you can change it

STOP DOING ... *No* makes way for *Yes*

GRATEFUL ... gratitude puts everything into perspective

Because ...

ADORED

Positive feelings are a form of power.

WEDNESDAY October 23, 2019 | *Sun enters Scorpio*

MY CORE DESIRED FEELINGS   *What I will do to feel the way I want to feel*

SCHEDULE ... joy expands time

: _____
: _____
: _____
: _____
: _____
: _____
: _____
: _____
: _____
: _____
: _____
: _____
: _____
: _____
: _____
: _____
: _____

TO-DO ... do what lights you up

1. _____
2. _____
3. _____
_____
_____
_____

BODY & WELLNESS My body is ...

DEVOTION I will dedicate this day to ...

NOT WORKING ... don't hold back

STOP DOING ... clarity is power

GRATEFUL ... note WHY you're grateful   *Because ...*

Thank your fear for the warning and move on.

CLEAN

THURSDAY October 24, 2019

MY CORE DESIRED FEELINGS

What I will do to feel the way I want to feel

SCHEDULE ... take up space

: _____
: _____
: _____
: _____
: _____
: _____
: _____
: _____
: _____
: _____
: _____
: _____
: _____
: _____
: _____
: _____

TO-DO ... believe in yourself

1. _____
2. _____
3. _____
   _____
   _____
   _____

BODY & WELLNESS My body is telling me ...

DEVOTION I will light a candle for ...

NOT WORKING ... claim it. Tame it.

STOP DOING ... don't take any crap

GRATEFUL ... be a beacon of optimism

Because ...

EMERGENT

Think of suffering as self-compassion school.

FRIDAY October 25, 2019

MY CORE DESIRED FEELINGS

What I will do to feel the way I want to feel

SCHEDULE ... what do you really want to happen?

: _____
: _____
: _____
: _____
: _____
: _____
: _____
: _____
: _____
: _____
: _____
: _____
: _____
: _____
: _____
: _____

TO-DO ... clarity creates simplicity

1. _____
2. _____
3. _____
_____
_____
_____

BODY & WELLNESS I will respect my body ...

DEVOTION I will have faith that ...

NOT WORKING ... feel free

STOP DOING ... freedom is your birthright

GRATEFUL ... specificity intensifies gratitude

Because ...

GLOWING

Honor your body and it will help you be even more creative.

SATURDAY October 26, 2019

MY CORE DESIRED FEELINGS

TO-DO ... visualize your ideal life

1. _____
2. _____
3. _____
_____
_____
_____

REFLECT
Which Core Desired Feeling seems farthest away? How do you feel about that?

SOUL PROMPT I need to have a good cry about

FIERCE

SUNDAY October 27, 2019
Diwali (Hindu) | ● *New Moon in Scorpio*

What I will do to feel the way I want to feel

TO-DO ... let it be easy

1. _____
2. _____
3. _____
_____
_____
_____

ENVISION
What would help you feel your Core Desired Feelings this week?

Have faith that you'll keep finding the light.

MONDAY October 28, 2019

MY CORE DESIRED FEELINGS   *What I will do to feel the way I want to feel*

SCHEDULE ... leave room for magic

: _____
: _____
: _____
: _____
: _____
: _____
: _____
: _____
: _____
: _____
: _____
: _____
: _____
: _____
: _____
: _____

TO-DO ... keep your soul on the agenda

1. _____
2. _____
3. _____
   _____
   _____
   _____

BODY & WELLNESS My body knows ...

DEVOTION Devotion creates miracles.

NOT WORKING ... does it feel light or heavy?

STOP DOING ... speak up

GRATEFUL ... ask for more   *Because ...*

ARTFUL

Comparison is a slippery slope to jealousy.

TUESDAY October 29, 2019

MY CORE DESIRED FEELINGS

What I will do to feel the way I want to feel

SCHEDULE ... work for Love

: _____
: _____
: _____
: _____
: _____
: _____
: _____
: _____
: _____
: _____
: _____
: _____
: _____
: _____
: _____
: _____

TO-DO ... make choices that liberate you

1. _____
2. _____
3. _____
   _____
   _____
   _____

BODY & WELLNESS I will tend to my body ...

DEVOTION I will contemplate ...

NOT WORKING ... name it so you can change it

STOP DOING ... *No* makes way for *Yes*

GRATEFUL ... gratitude puts everything into perspective

Because ...

AMBITIOUS

Only seek to be more of yourself.

WEDNESDAY October 30, 2019

MY CORE DESIRED FEELINGS

What I will do to feel the way I want to feel

SCHEDULE ... simplicity is freedom

: _____
: _____
: _____
: _____
: _____
: _____
: _____
: _____
: _____
: _____
: _____
: _____
: _____
: _____
: _____
: _____

TO-DO ... imagine

1. _____
2. _____
3. _____
   _____
   _____
   _____

BODY & WELLNESS I will nourish my body ...

DEVOTION I will pray for (who/what) ...

NOT WORKING ... don't hold back

STOP DOING ... clarity is power

GRATEFUL ... note WHY you're grateful

Because ...

You will be misunderstood. Proceed anyway.

BELOVED

THURSDAY October 31, 2019 | *Halloween/Samhain (Pagan) | Mercury stations Retrograde in Scorpio*

MY CORE DESIRED FEELINGS

What I will do to feel the way I want to feel

SCHEDULE ... does it light you up?

: _____
: _____
: _____
: _____
: _____
: _____
: _____
: _____
: _____
: _____
: _____
: _____
: _____
: _____
: _____
: _____
: _____

TO-DO ... prioritize pleasure

1. _____
2. _____
3. _____
_____
_____
_____

BODY & WELLNESS My body helps me ...

DEVOTION My meditation will be ...

NOT WORKING ... claim it. Tame it.

STOP DOING ... don't take any crap

GRATEFUL ... be a beacon of optimism

Because ...

AUDACIOUS

You are profoundly, incomprehensibly unique.

IDEAS. DESIRES. WISDOM. ... know what brings you back to center

THE PAST MONTH: Reflect. Clarify. Create.

BE DELIBERATE.
Every feeling you experience is a beacon for more of the same feeling. So keep shifting your consciousness back to your Core Desired Feelings. It's an ebb and flow, a constantly creative experience that you are driving. On track... get off track. Choose how you want to feel and get back on track.

MY CORE DESIRED FEELINGS
My CDFs are strongest in... I feel most aligned with... I'm moving toward...
I want to give more attention to...

MY GOALS & INTENTIONS
My goals are bringing my CDFs to life... I need to change up, refine or deepen...
To move closer to my goals & intentions I...

WHAT'S REALLY WORKING, YA!
I really felt [your CDF] when... This month I was so brilliant...
I created... I felt... I allowed... I accomplished...

WHAT NEEDS TO SHIFT
I felt disappointed... The challenge...

THE NEW MONTH: Envision. Intend. Energize.

SPEAK OF WHAT YOU DESIRE.
"To burn with desire and keep quiet about it is the greatest punishment we can bring on ourselves."
— Federico García Lorca

HOW I WILL
be stronger… softer… more determined… less uptight… more flexible… less constricted… more open… less accommodating… more accommodating… less worried… more generous… less doubtful… more trusting… less punishing… more pleasure-creating… less fearful… more loving…

TO MOVE TOWARD MY GOALS & INTENTIONS…

NOVEMBER
2019

MONDAY	TUESDAY	WEDNESDAY
WEEK 44		
4	5	6
WEEK 45		
Veterans Day (US) **Remembrance Day (CAN, AUS)** 11	○ Full Moon in Taurus 12	13
WEEK 46		
Mars enters Scorpio 18	19	Mercury stations Direct in Scorpio 20
WEEK 47		
International Day for Eliminating Violence Against Women 25 Venus enters Capricorn	● New Moon in Sagittarius 26	Neptune stations Direct in Pisces 27
WEEK 48		

I'm sorry. Please forgive me. Thank you. I love you.

This is the Ho'oponopono Prayer for reconciliation and forgiveness. Recite this prayer seven times and feel the radiance of the prayer washing away your old pain.

NOVEMBER

THURSDAY	FRIDAY	SATURDAY	SUNDAY
	Venus enters Sagittarius 1	2	**Daylight Saving Time ends (CAN, US)** 3
7	8	9	**Mawlid (Islam)** 10
14	15	16	17
21	Sun enters Sagittarius 22	23	24
Thanksgiving Day (US) 28	29	30	

NOVEMBER

FRIDAY November 1, 2019 | *Venus enters Sagittarius*

MY CORE DESIRED FEELINGS

What I will do to feel the way I want to feel

SCHEDULE ... joy expands time

: _____
: _____
: _____
: _____
: _____
: _____
: _____
: _____
: _____
: _____
: _____
: _____
: _____
: _____
: _____
: _____

TO-DO ... do what lights you up

1. _____
2. _____
3. _____
   _____
   _____
   _____

BODY & WELLNESS My body is ...

DEVOTION I will dedicate this day to ...

NOT WORKING ... feel free

STOP DOING ... freedom is your birthright

GRATEFUL ... specificity intensifies gratitude

Because ...

LOYAL

Let your voice ride on your breath.

SATURDAY November 2, 2019

MY CORE DESIRED FEELINGS

TO-DO ... make space for the light to enter

1. _____
2. _____
3. _____
   _____
   _____
   _____

REFLECT
When you are feeling your CDFs, how does that help you be of more service to others?

SUNDAY November 3, 2019
Daylight Saving Time ends (CAN, US)

What I will do to feel the way I want to feel

TO-DO ... what would be comforting?

1. _____
2. _____
3. _____
   _____
   _____
   _____

ENVISION
How will you show up in the world as one of your CDFs?

SOUL PROMPT I worship

The surest way to simplify your life is to focus on what matters most.

SOVEREIGN

MONDAY November 4, 2019

MY CORE DESIRED FEELINGS

What I will do to feel the way I want to feel

SCHEDULE ... take up space

: _____
: _____
: _____
: _____
: _____
: _____
: _____
: _____
: _____
: _____
: _____
: _____
: _____
: _____
: _____
: _____
: _____

TO-DO ... believe in yourself

1. _____
2. _____
3. _____
   _____
   _____
   _____

BODY & WELLNESS My body is telling me ...

DEVOTION I will light a candle for ...

NOT WORKING ... does it feel light or heavy?

STOP DOING ... speak up

GRATEFUL ... ask for more

Because ...

LIFE-GIVING

you are the center of your universe

TUESDAY November 5, 2019

MY CORE DESIRED FEELINGS

What I will do to feel the way I want to feel

SCHEDULE ... what do you really want to happen?

: _____
: _____
: _____
: _____
: _____
: _____
: _____
: _____
: _____
: _____
: _____
: _____
: _____
: _____
: _____
: _____

TO-DO ... clarity creates simplicity

1. _____
2. _____
3. _____
_____
_____
_____

BODY & WELLNESS I will respect my body ...

DEVOTION I will have faith that ...

NOT WORKING ... name it so you can change it

STOP DOING ... *No* makes way for *Yes*

GRATEFUL ... gratitude puts everything into perspective

Because ...

Don't hold back.

MYSTICAL

WEDNESDAY November 6, 2019

MY CORE DESIRED FEELINGS

What I will do to feel the way I want to feel

SCHEDULE ... leave room for magic

: _____
: _____
: _____
: _____
: _____
: _____
: _____
: _____
: _____
: _____
: _____
: _____
: _____
: _____
: _____
: _____

TO-DO ... keep your soul on the agenda

1. _____
2. _____
3. _____
   _____
   _____
   _____

BODY & WELLNESS My body knows ...

DEVOTION Devotion creates miracles.

NOT WORKING ... don't hold back

STOP DOING ... clarity is power

GRATEFUL ... note WHY you're grateful

Because ...

TRIUMPHANT

It won't change until you admit to the pain.

THURSDAY November 7, 2019

MY CORE DESIRED FEELINGS   *What I will do to feel the way I want to feel*

SCHEDULE ... work for Love   **TO-DO** ... make choices that liberate you

: _____   1. _____
: _____   2. _____
: _____   3. _____
: _____   _____
: _____   _____
: _____   _____
: _____
: _____   **BODY & WELLNESS** I will tend to my body ...
: _____
: _____   **DEVOTION** I will contemplate ...
: _____
: _____
: _____   **NOT WORKING** ... claim it. Tame it.
: _____
: _____   **STOP DOING** ... don't take any crap
: _____
: _____

GRATEFUL ... be a beacon of optimism   *Because ...*

Prove them wrong for all the right reasons.

EVOLUTION

FRIDAY November 8, 2019

MY CORE DESIRED FEELINGS

What I will do to feel the way I want to feel

SCHEDULE ... simplicity is freedom

: _____
: _____
: _____
: _____
: _____
: _____
: _____
: _____
: _____
: _____
: _____
: _____
: _____
: _____

TO-DO ... imagine

1. _____
2. _____
3. _____
   _____
   _____

BODY & WELLNESS I will nourish my body ...

DEVOTION I will pray for (who/what) ...

NOT WORKING ... feel free

STOP DOING ... freedom is your birthright

GRATEFUL ... specificity intensifies gratitude

Because ...

RECEPTIVE

The universe Loves a believer.

SATURDAY November 9, 2019

MY CORE DESIRED FEELINGS

TO-DO ... relax ... rebel ... rest

1. _____
2. _____
3. _____
   _____
   _____
   _____

REFLECT
Have a conversation with one of your CDFs, ask it to give you some guidance.

SUNDAY November 10, 2019
Mawlid (Islam)

What I will do to feel the way I want to feel

TO-DO ... visualize your ideal life

1. _____
2. _____
3. _____
   _____
   _____
   _____

ENVISION
What spaces or places embody your Core Desired Feelings?

SOUL PROMPT My most regular waking thought is

Identify with light.

HEALTHY

MONDAY November 11, 2019 | *Veterans Day (US) | Remembrance Day (CAN, AUS)*

MY CORE DESIRED FEELINGS   *What I will do to feel the way I want to feel*

SCHEDULE ... does it light you up?

: _____
: _____
: _____
: _____
: _____
: _____
: _____
: _____
: _____
: _____
: _____
: _____
: _____
: _____
: _____
: _____

TO-DO ... prioritize pleasure

1. _____
2. _____
3. _____
   _____
   _____
   _____

BODY & WELLNESS My body helps me ...

DEVOTION My meditation will be ...

NOT WORKING ... does it feel light or heavy?

STOP DOING ... speak up

GRATEFUL ... ask for more   *Because ...*

REAL

Renew your vows.

TUESDAY November 12, 2019 | ○ *Full Moon in Taurus*

MY CORE DESIRED FEELINGS   *What I will do to feel the way I want to feel*

SCHEDULE ... joy expands time

_:_ _____
_:_ _____
_:_ _____
_:_ _____
_:_ _____
_:_ _____
_:_ _____
_:_ _____
_:_ _____
_:_ _____
_:_ _____
_:_ _____
_:_ _____
_:_ _____
_:_ _____

TO-DO ... do what lights you up

1. _____
2. _____
3. _____
_____
_____
_____

BODY & WELLNESS My body is ...

DEVOTION I will dedicate this day to ...

NOT WORKING ... name it so you can change it

STOP DOING ... *No* makes way for *Yes*

GRATEFUL ... gratitude puts everything into perspective   *Because ...*

What makes you feel real?

CHEERFUL

WEDNESDAY November 13, 2019

MY CORE DESIRED FEELINGS

What I will do to feel the way I want to feel

SCHEDULE ... take up space

: _____
: _____
: _____
: _____
: _____
: _____
: _____
: _____
: _____
: _____
: _____
: _____
: _____
: _____
: _____
: _____

TO-DO ... believe in yourself

1. _____
2. _____
3. _____
   _____
   _____

BODY & WELLNESS My body is telling me ...

DEVOTION I will light a candle for ...

NOT WORKING ... don't hold back

STOP DOING ... clarity is power

GRATEFUL ... note WHY you're grateful

Because ...

TRANQUIL

The only thing that you really have control over is your feelings.

THURSDAY November 14, 2019

MY CORE DESIRED FEELINGS   *What I will do to feel the way I want to feel*

SCHEDULE ... what do you really want to happen?   **TO-DO** ... clarity creates simplicity

: _____   1. _____
: _____   2. _____
: _____   3. _____
: _____   _____
: _____   _____
: _____   _____

: _____   **BODY & WELLNESS** I will respect my body ...

: _____
: _____   **DEVOTION** I will have faith that ...

: _____
: _____   **NOT WORKING** ... claim it. Tame it.

: _____
: _____   **STOP DOING** ... don't take any crap

: _____
: _____

GRATEFUL ... be a beacon of optimism   *Because ...*

Energy follows thought.

FUN

FRIDAY November 15, 2019

MY CORE DESIRED FEELINGS

What I will do to feel the way I want to feel

SCHEDULE ... leave room for magic

: _____
: _____
: _____
: _____
: _____
: _____
: _____
: _____
: _____
: _____
: _____
: _____
: _____
: _____
: _____
: _____

TO-DO ... keep your soul on the agenda

1. _____
2. _____
3. _____
   _____
   _____
   _____

BODY & WELLNESS My body knows ...

DEVOTION Devotion creates miracles.

NOT WORKING ... feel free

STOP DOING ... freedom is your birthright

GRATEFUL ... specificity intensifies gratitude

Because ...

OF SERVICE

If you declare that you'll figure it out, the possibilities are endless.

SATURDAY November 16, 2019

MY CORE DESIRED FEELINGS

TO-DO ... let it be easy

1. _____
2. _____
3. _____
_____
_____
_____

REFLECT
Hands on your heart, eyes closed, recite your CDFs and see what images arise.

SUNDAY November 17, 2019

What I will do to feel the way I want to feel

TO-DO ... make space for the light to enter

1. _____
2. _____
3. _____
_____
_____
_____

ENVISION
What Core Desired Feeling(s) need extra attention this week?

SOUL PROMPT I'm all for

Consider everything you've ever been thanked for.

INTENTIONAL

MONDAY November 18, 2019 | *Mars enters Scorpio*

MY CORE DESIRED FEELINGS   *What I will do to feel the way I want to feel*

SCHEDULE ... work for Love

: _____
: _____
: _____
: _____
: _____
: _____
: _____
: _____
: _____
: _____
: _____
: _____
: _____
: _____
: _____
: _____

TO-DO ... make choices that liberate you

1. _____
2. _____
3. _____
   _____
   _____
   _____

BODY & WELLNESS I will tend to my body ...

DEVOTION I will contemplate ...

NOT WORKING ... does it feel light or heavy?

STOP DOING ... speak up

GRATEFUL ... ask for more   *Because ...*

COURAGE

You have the resolve to find your resolve.

TUESDAY November 19, 2019

MY CORE DESIRED FEELINGS   *What I will do to feel the way I want to feel*

SCHEDULE ... simplicity is freedom   **TO-DO** ... imagine

: _____   1. _____
: _____   2. _____
: _____   3. _____
: _____   _____
: _____   _____
: _____   _____
: _____   **BODY & WELLNESS** I will nourish my body ...
: _____
: _____   **DEVOTION** I will pray for (who/what) ...
: _____
: _____   **NOT WORKING** ... name it so you can change it
: _____
: _____   **STOP DOING** ... *No* makes way for *Yes*
: _____
: _____

GRATEFUL ... gratitude puts everything into perspective   *Because ...*

The deeper your self love, the greater your protection.

NOBLE

WEDNESDAY November 20, 2019 | *Mercury stations Direct in Scorpio*

MY CORE DESIRED FEELINGS   *What I will do to feel the way I want to feel*

SCHEDULE ... does it light you up?

: _____
: _____
: _____
: _____
: _____
: _____
: _____
: _____
: _____
: _____
: _____
: _____
: _____
: _____
: _____
: _____

TO-DO ... prioritize pleasure

1. _____
2. _____
3. _____
  _____
  _____
  _____

BODY & WELLNESS My body helps me ...

DEVOTION My meditation will be ...

NOT WORKING ... don't hold back

STOP DOING ... clarity is power

GRATEFUL ... note WHY you're grateful   *Because ...*

INFLUENTIAL

Your soul is the Love of all Loves.

THURSDAY November 21, 2019

MY CORE DESIRED FEELINGS   *What I will do to feel the way I want to feel*

SCHEDULE ... joy expands time

: _____
: _____
: _____
: _____
: _____
: _____
: _____
: _____
: _____
: _____
: _____
: _____
: _____
: _____
: _____
: _____
: _____

TO-DO ... do what lights you up

1. _____
2. _____
3. _____
   _____
   _____
   _____

BODY & WELLNESS My body is ...

DEVOTION I will dedicate this day to ...

NOT WORKING ... claim it. Tame it.

STOP DOING ... don't take any crap

GRATEFUL ... be a beacon of optimism   *Because ...*

Love what you see.

ENDLESS

FRIDAY November 22, 2019 | *Sun enters Sagittarius*

MY CORE DESIRED FEELINGS

What I will do to feel the way I want to feel

SCHEDULE ... take up space

: _____
: _____
: _____
: _____
: _____
: _____
: _____
: _____
: _____
: _____
: _____
: _____
: _____
: _____
: _____
: _____

TO-DO ... believe in yourself

1. _____
2. _____
3. _____
   _____
   _____
   _____

BODY & WELLNESS My body is telling me ...

DEVOTION I will light a candle for ...

NOT WORKING ... feel free

STOP DOING ... freedom is your birthright

GRATEFUL ... specificity intensifies gratitude

Because ...

COMMUNITY

Contrast is an excellent teacher.

SATURDAY November 23, 2019

MY CORE DESIRED FEELINGS

TO-DO ... what would be comforting?

1. _____
2. _____
3. _____

_____
_____
_____

REFLECT
The Core Desired Feeling closest to my heart is...

SUNDAY November 24, 2019

What I will do to feel the way I want to feel

TO-DO ... relax ... rebel ... rest

1. _____
2. _____
3. _____

_____
_____
_____

ENVISION
How are your Core Desired Feelings experienced in your body?

SOUL PROMPT Two beautiful experiences

First thought, right answer.

MONDAY November 25, 2019 | *International Day for Eliminating Violence Against Women*
Venus enters Capricorn

MY CORE DESIRED FEELINGS   *What I will do to feel the way I want to feel*

SCHEDULE ... what do you really want to happen?

: _____
: _____
: _____
: _____
: _____
: _____
: _____
: _____
: _____
: _____
: _____
: _____
: _____
: _____
: _____
: _____

TO-DO ... clarity creates simplicity

1. _____
2. _____
3. _____
   _____
   _____
   _____

BODY & WELLNESS I will respect my body ...

DEVOTION I will have faith that ...

NOT WORKING ... does it feel light or heavy?

STOP DOING ... speak up

GRATEFUL ... ask for more   *Because ...*

BLOOMING

Time doesn't heal. Consciousness does.

//
TUESDAY November 26, 2019 | ● *New Moon in Sagittarius*

MY CORE DESIRED FEELINGS *What I will do to feel the way I want to feel*

SCHEDULE ... leave room for magic

: _____
: _____
: _____
: _____
: _____
: _____
: _____
: _____
: _____
: _____
: _____
: _____
: _____
: _____
: _____
: _____

TO-DO ... keep your soul on the agenda

1. _____
2. _____
3. _____
   _____
   _____
   _____

BODY & WELLNESS My body knows ...

DEVOTION Devotion creates miracles.

NOT WORKING ... name it so you can change it

STOP DOING ... *No* makes way for *Yes*

GRATEFUL ... gratitude puts everything into perspective   *Because ...*

The easy way = more time to enjoy what you've got, and to get more of what you want.

GODDESS

WEDNESDAY November 27, 2019 | *Neptune stations Direct in Pisces*

MY CORE DESIRED FEELINGS

What I will do to feel the way I want to feel

SCHEDULE ... work for Love

   : _____
   : _____
   : _____
   : _____
   : _____
   : _____
   : _____
   : _____
   : _____
   : _____
   : _____
   : _____
   : _____
   : _____
   : _____
   : _____

TO-DO ... make choices that liberate you

1. _____
2. _____
3. _____

BODY & WELLNESS I will tend to my body ...

DEVOTION I will contemplate ...

NOT WORKING ... don't hold back

STOP DOING ... clarity is power

GRATEFUL ... note WHY you're grateful

Because ...

SEEN

Even in your despair, you are magnificent.

THURSDAY November 28, 2019 | *Thanksgiving Day (US)*

MY CORE DESIRED FEELINGS   *What I will do to feel the way I want to feel*

SCHEDULE ... simplicity is freedom

: _____
: _____
: _____
: _____
: _____
: _____
: _____
: _____
: _____
: _____
: _____
: _____
: _____
: _____
: _____
: _____

TO-DO ... imagine

1. _____
2. _____
3. _____
   _____
   _____
   _____

BODY & WELLNESS I will nourish my body ...

DEVOTION I will pray for (who/what) ...

NOT WORKING ... claim it. Tame it.

STOP DOING ... don't take any crap

GRATEFUL ... be a beacon of optimism   *Because ...*

You think you need an architect but you are already the temple.

RENEWED

FRIDAY November 29, 2019

MY CORE DESIRED FEELINGS

What I will do to feel the way I want to feel

SCHEDULE ... does it light you up?

   : _____
   : _____
   : _____
   : _____
   : _____
   : _____
   : _____
   : _____
   : _____
   : _____
   : _____
   : _____
   : _____
   : _____
   : _____

TO-DO ... prioritize pleasure

1. _____
2. _____
3. _____
    _____
    _____

BODY & WELLNESS My body helps me ...

DEVOTION My meditation will be ...

NOT WORKING ... feel free

STOP DOING ... freedom is your birthright

GRATEFUL ... specificity intensifies gratitude

Because ...

BEAUTY

What becomes possible when you say No?

SATURDAY November 30, 2019

MY CORE DESIRED FEELINGS

What I will do to feel the way I want to feel

TO-DO ... visualize your ideal life

1. _____
2. _____
3. _____
_____
_____
_____

TO-DO ... let it be easy

1. _____
2. _____
3. _____
_____
_____
_____

REFLECT
A prayer: Thank you for the clarity and courage to make choices that favor my Core Desired Feelings.

ENVISION
A prayer: Thank you for guiding me to express and experience my Core Desired Feelings.

SOUL PROMPT I give myself permission to

Unhook. Return the hook to where it came from.

RELAXED

THE PAST MONTH: Reflect. Clarify. Create.

GO THERE.
When you can respect the darkness within yourself without any guilt trips, you're becoming truly free. And by facing it, you can bring it out into the light for healing and transmutation.

MY CORE DESIRED FEELINGS
My CDFs are strongest in… I feel most aligned with… I'm moving toward…
I want to give more attention to…

MY GOALS & INTENTIONS
My goals are bringing my CDFs to life… I need to change up, refine or deepen…
To move closer to my goals & intentions I…

WHAT'S REALLY WORKING, YA!
I really felt [your CDF] when… This month I was so brilliant…
I created… I felt… I allowed… I accomplished…

WHAT NEEDS TO SHIFT
I felt disappointed… The challenge…

THE NEW MONTH: Envision. Intend. Energize.

BE THE EXCEPTION.
"A strong spirit transcends rules."
— Prince

HOW I WILL
be stronger… softer… more determined… less uptight… more flexible… less constricted… more open… less accommodating… more accommodating… less worried… more generous… less doubtful… more trusting… less punishing… more pleasure-creating… less fearful… more loving…

TO MOVE TOWARD MY GOALS & INTENTIONS…

DECEMBER
2019

MONDAY	TUESDAY	WEDNESDAY
WEEK 48		
Jupiter enters Capricorn 2	3	4
WEEK 49		
Mercury enters Sagittarius 9	10	○ Full Moon in Gemini 11
WEEK 50		
16	17	18
WEEK 51		
23	**Christmas Eve** 24	**Christmas Day** 25 ● New Moon in Capricorn
WEEK 52		
Chanukah/Hanukkah ends - evening (Jewish holiday) 30	**New Year's Eve** 31	
WEEK 1		

May the long time sun shine upon you, All Love surround you, And the pure light within you, Guide your way on.

An Irish Blessing used as a farewell in Kundalini yoga. Give it away over and over.

THURSDAY	FRIDAY	SATURDAY	SUNDAY
			1
5	6	7	8
12	13	14	15
Venus enters Aquarius 19	20	**Winter Solstice/Yule (Pagan)** 21 Sun enters Capricorn	**Chanukah/Hanukkah begins - evening (Jewish holiday)** 22
Boxing Day (CAN, AUS) 26 Annular Solar Eclipse	27	Mercury enters Capricorn 28	29

DECEMBER

SUNDAY December 1, 2019

MY CORE DESIRED FEELINGS

What I will do to feel the way I want to feel

TO-DO ... make space for the light to enter

1. _____
2. _____
3. _____

_____
_____
_____

TO-DO ... what would be comforting?

1. _____
2. _____
3. _____

_____
_____
_____

REFLECT
What Core Desired Feeling felt most alive in your life? Why/how?

ENVISION
What rituals support your Core Desired Feelings?

SOUL PROMPT I give myself permission to

FREE

Turn your longing into a calling.

MONDAY December 2, 2019 | *Jupiter enters Capricorn*

MY CORE DESIRED FEELINGS   *What I will do to feel the way I want to feel*

SCHEDULE ... joy expands time   **TO-DO** ... do what lights you up

  : _____   1. _____
  : _____   2. _____
  : _____   3. _____
  : _____   _____
  : _____   _____
  : _____   _____

  : _____   **BODY & WELLNESS** My body is ...
  : _____
  : _____   **DEVOTION** I will dedicate this day to ...
  : _____
  : _____
  : _____   **NOT WORKING** ... does it feel light or heavy?
  : _____
  : _____
  : _____   **STOP DOING** ... speak up
  : _____
  : _____

GRATEFUL ... ask for more   *Because ...*

You have to Love the you that you outgrew.

BRILLIANT

TUESDAY December 3, 2019

MY CORE DESIRED FEELINGS

What I will do to feel the way I want to feel

SCHEDULE ... take up space

: _____
: _____
: _____
: _____
: _____
: _____
: _____
: _____
: _____
: _____
: _____
: _____
: _____
: _____
: _____
: _____
: _____

TO-DO ... believe in yourself

1. _____
2. _____
3. _____
   _____
   _____

BODY & WELLNESS My body is telling me ...

DEVOTION I will light a candle for ...

NOT WORKING ... name it so you can change it

STOP DOING ... *No* makes way for *Yes*

GRATEFUL ... gratitude puts everything into perspective

Because ...

SECURE

Hang out with people you can easily adore, or at least respect.

WEDNESDAY December 4, 2019

MY CORE DESIRED FEELINGS   *What I will do to feel the way I want to feel*

SCHEDULE ... what do you really want to happen?

: _____
: _____
: _____
: _____
: _____
: _____
: _____
: _____
: _____
: _____
: _____
: _____
: _____
: _____
: _____
: _____
: _____

TO-DO ... clarity creates simplicity

1. _____
2. _____
3. _____
   _____
   _____
   _____

BODY & WELLNESS I will respect my body ...

DEVOTION I will have faith that ...

NOT WORKING ... don't hold back

STOP DOING ... clarity is power

GRATEFUL ... note WHY you're grateful   *Because ...*

Bliss. Anger. Gentleness. Grief. Desperation. Joy. Joy. Joy. All in one day.

ABSTRACT

THURSDAY December 5, 2019

MY CORE DESIRED FEELINGS

What I will do to feel the way I want to feel

SCHEDULE ... leave room for magic

: _____
: _____
: _____
: _____
: _____
: _____
: _____
: _____
: _____
: _____
: _____
: _____
: _____
: _____
: _____
: _____
: _____

TO-DO ... keep your soul on the agenda

1. _____
2. _____
3. _____
   _____
   _____
   _____

BODY & WELLNESS My body knows ...

DEVOTION Devotion creates miracles.

NOT WORKING ... claim it. Tame it.

STOP DOING ... don't take any crap

GRATEFUL ... be a beacon of optimism

Because ...

APPRECIATED

Healing for one is healing for many.

FRIDAY December 6, 2019

MY CORE DESIRED FEELINGS *What I will do to feel the way I want to feel*

SCHEDULE ... work for Love

: _____
: _____
: _____
: _____
: _____
: _____
: _____
: _____
: _____
: _____
: _____
: _____
: _____
: _____
: _____
: _____
: _____

TO-DO ... make choices that liberate you

1. _____
2. _____
3. _____
_____
_____
_____

BODY & WELLNESS I will tend to my body ...

DEVOTION I will contemplate ...

NOT WORKING ... feel free

STOP DOING ... freedom is your birthright

GRATEFUL ... specificity intensifies gratitude   *Because ...*

Do your work in the world.

ORGANIC

SATURDAY December 7, 2019

MY CORE DESIRED FEELINGS

TO-DO ... relax ... rebel ... rest

1. _____
2. _____
3. _____
_____
_____
_____

REFLECT
Which Core Desired Feeling seems farthest away? How do you feel about that?

SOUL PROMPT Five beautiful things I can see right now

SUNDAY December 8, 2019

What I will do to feel the way I want to feel

TO-DO ... visualize your ideal life

1. _____
2. _____
3. _____
_____
_____
_____

ENVISION
What would help you feel your Core Desired Feelings this week?

NATURAL

Practice good manners with yourself.

MONDAY December 9, 2019 | *Mercury enters Sagittarius*

MY CORE DESIRED FEELINGS   *What I will do to feel the way I want to feel*

SCHEDULE ... simplicity is freedom

TO-DO ... imagine
1.
2.
3.

BODY & WELLNESS I will nourish my body ...

DEVOTION I will pray for (who/what) ...

NOT WORKING ... does it feel light or heavy?

STOP DOING ... speak up

GRATEFUL ... ask for more   *Because ...*

Conformity sucks.

BRAVE

TUESDAY December 10, 2019

MY CORE DESIRED FEELINGS

What I will do to feel the way I want to feel

SCHEDULE ... does it light you up?

: _____
: _____
: _____
: _____
: _____
: _____
: _____
: _____
: _____
: _____
: _____
: _____
: _____
: _____
: _____
: _____

TO-DO ... prioritize pleasure

1. _____
2. _____
3. _____
   _____
   _____

BODY & WELLNESS My body helps me ...

DEVOTION My meditation will be ...

NOT WORKING ... name it so you can change it

STOP DOING ... *No* makes way for *Yes*

GRATEFUL ... gratitude puts everything into perspective

Because ...

UNMATCHED

Worship your vision.

WEDNESDAY December 11, 2019 | ○ *Full Moon in Gemini*

MY CORE DESIRED FEELINGS *What I will do to feel the way I want to feel*

SCHEDULE ... joy expands time

: _____
: _____
: _____
: _____
: _____
: _____
: _____
: _____
: _____
: _____
: _____
: _____
: _____
: _____
: _____
: _____
: _____

TO-DO ... do what lights you up

1. _____
2. _____
3. _____
   _____
   _____
   _____

BODY & WELLNESS My body is ...

DEVOTION I will dedicate this day to ...

NOT WORKING ... don't hold back

STOP DOING ... clarity is power

GRATEFUL ... note WHY you're grateful *Because ...*

Bring your holy mouth to Love and ask for what you want.

DELIBERATE

THURSDAY December 12, 2019

MY CORE DESIRED FEELINGS

What I will do to feel the way I want to feel

SCHEDULE ... take up space

: _____
: _____
: _____
: _____
: _____
: _____
: _____
: _____
: _____
: _____
: _____
: _____
: _____
: _____
: _____
: _____

TO-DO ... believe in yourself

1. _____
2. _____
3. _____
   _____
   _____
   _____

BODY & WELLNESS My body is telling me ...

DEVOTION I will light a candle for ...

NOT WORKING ... claim it. Tame it.

STOP DOING ... don't take any crap

GRATEFUL ... be a beacon of optimism

Because ...

SEDUCTIVE

Be still with yourself.

FRIDAY December 13, 2019

MY CORE DESIRED FEELINGS

What I will do to feel the way I want to feel

SCHEDULE ... what do you really want to happen?

: _____
: _____
: _____
: _____
: _____
: _____
: _____
: _____
: _____
: _____
: _____
: _____
: _____
: _____
: _____
: _____

TO-DO ... clarity creates simplicity

1. _____
2. _____
3. _____
_____
_____
_____

BODY & WELLNESS I will respect my body ...

DEVOTION I will have faith that ...

NOT WORKING ... feel free

STOP DOING ... freedom is your birthright

GRATEFUL ... specificity intensifies gratitude

Because ...

Empathy is the great healer.

DYNAMIC

SATURDAY December 14, 2019

MY CORE DESIRED FEELINGS

TO-DO ... let it be easy

1. _____
2. _____
3. _____
   _____
   _____
   _____

REFLECT
When you are feeling your CDFs, how does that help you be of more service to others?

SOUL PROMPT I am most looking forward to

TANGIBLE

SUNDAY December 15, 2019

What I will do to feel the way I want to feel

TO-DO ... make space for the light to enter

1. _____
2. _____
3. _____
   _____
   _____
   _____

ENVISION
How will you show up in the world as one of your CDFs?

Make stuff that feels good to make.

MONDAY December 16, 2019

MY CORE DESIRED FEELINGS

What I will do to feel the way I want to feel

SCHEDULE ... leave room for magic

: _____
: _____
: _____
: _____
: _____
: _____
: _____
: _____
: _____
: _____
: _____
: _____
: _____
: _____
: _____
: _____

TO-DO ... keep your soul on the agenda

1. _____
2. _____
3. _____
   _____
   _____
   _____

BODY & WELLNESS My body knows ...

DEVOTION Devotion creates miracles.

NOT WORKING ... does it feel light or heavy?

STOP DOING ... speak up

GRATEFUL ... ask for more

Because ...

ROMANCE

Stream your consciousness.

TUESDAY December 17, 2019

MY CORE DESIRED FEELINGS

What I will do to feel the way I want to feel

SCHEDULE ... work for Love

: _____
: _____
: _____
: _____
: _____
: _____
: _____
: _____
: _____
: _____
: _____
: _____
: _____
: _____
: _____
: _____
: _____

TO-DO ... make choices that liberate you

1. _____
2. _____
3. _____
   _____
   _____

BODY & WELLNESS I will tend to my body ...

DEVOTION I will contemplate ...

NOT WORKING ... name it so you can change it

STOP DOING ... *No* makes way for *Yes*

GRATEFUL ... gratitude puts everything into perspective

Because ...

SOUL CENTERED

Disrupt normalcy.

WEDNESDAY December 18, 2019

MY CORE DESIRED FEELINGS

What I will do to feel the way I want to feel

SCHEDULE ... simplicity is freedom

: _____
: _____
: _____
: _____
: _____
: _____
: _____
: _____
: _____
: _____
: _____
: _____
: _____
: _____
: _____
: _____

TO-DO ... imagine

1. _____
2. _____
3. _____
_____
_____
_____

BODY & WELLNESS I will nourish my body ...

DEVOTION I will pray for (who/what) ...

NOT WORKING ... don't hold back

STOP DOING ... clarity is power

GRATEFUL ... note WHY you're grateful

Because ...

Compassion illuminates the darkness.

CLARITY

THURSDAY December 19, 2019 | *Venus enters Aquarius*

MY CORE DESIRED FEELINGS

What I will do to feel the way I want to feel

SCHEDULE ... does it light you up?

: _____
: _____
: _____
: _____
: _____
: _____
: _____
: _____
: _____
: _____
: _____
: _____
: _____
: _____
: _____
: _____

TO-DO ... prioritize pleasure

1. _____
2. _____
3. _____
   _____
   _____
   _____

BODY & WELLNESS My body helps me ...

DEVOTION My meditation will be ...

NOT WORKING ... claim it. Tame it.

STOP DOING ... don't take any crap

GRATEFUL ... be a beacon of optimism

Because ...

TUNED-IN

Destruction before Creation

FRIDAY December 20, 2019

MY CORE DESIRED FEELINGS

What I will do to feel the way I want to feel

SCHEDULE ... joy expands time

: _____
: _____
: _____
: _____
: _____
: _____
: _____
: _____
: _____
: _____
: _____
: _____
: _____
: _____
: _____

TO-DO ... do what lights you up

1. _____
2. _____
3. _____
   _____
   _____
   _____

BODY & WELLNESS My body is ...

DEVOTION I will dedicate this day to ...

NOT WORKING ... feel free

STOP DOING ... freedom is your birthright

GRATEFUL ... specificity intensifies gratitude

Because ...

You are the guru.

ON PURPOSE

SATURDAY December 21, 2019
Winter Solstice/Yule (Pagan)
Sun enters Capricorn

MY CORE DESIRE FEELINGS

TO-DO ... what would be comforting?

1. _____
2. _____
3. _____

_____
_____
_____

REFLECT
Have a conversation with one of your CDFs, ask it to give you some guidance.

SOUL PROMPT Five words about money

SUNDAY December 22, 2019
Chanukah/Hanukkah begins - evening (Jewish holiday)

What I will do to feel the way I want to feel

TO-DO ... relax ... rebel ... rest

1. _____
2. _____
3. _____

_____
_____
_____

ENVISION
What spaces or places embody your Core Desired Feelings?

RECOGNIZED

Nothing changes without you.

MONDAY December 23, 2019

MY CORE DESIRED FEELINGS   *What I will do to feel the way I want to feel*

SCHEDULE ... take up space

: _____
: _____
: _____
: _____
: _____
: _____
: _____
: _____
: _____
: _____
: _____
: _____
: _____
: _____
: _____
: _____

TO-DO ... believe in yourself

1. _____
2. _____
3. _____
_____
_____
_____

BODY & WELLNESS My body is telling me ...

DEVOTION I will light a candle for ...

NOT WORKING ... does it feel light or heavy?

STOP DOING ... speak up

GRATEFUL ... ask for more   *Because ...*

So much suffering is optional.

PASSIONATE

TUESDAY December 24, 2019 | *Christmas Eve*

MY CORE DESIRED FEELINGS

What I will do to feel the way I want to feel

SCHEDULE ... what do you really want to happen?

: _____
: _____
: _____
: _____
: _____
: _____
: _____
: _____
: _____
: _____
: _____
: _____
: _____
: _____
: _____
: _____

TO-DO ... clarity creates simplicity

1. _____
2. _____
3. _____
   _____
   _____
   _____

BODY & WELLNESS I will respect my body ...

DEVOTION I will have faith that ...

NOT WORKING ... name it so you can change it

STOP DOING ... *No* makes way for *Yes*

GRATEFUL ... gratitude puts everything into perspective

Because ...

BRIMMING

Use the intelligence of your heart.

WEDNESDAY December 25, 2019 | *Christmas Day* | ● *New Moon in Capricorn*

MY CORE DESIRED FEELINGS   *What I will do to feel the way I want to feel*

SCHEDULE ... leave room for magic

: _____
: _____
: _____
: _____
: _____
: _____
: _____
: _____
: _____
: _____
: _____
: _____
: _____
: _____
: _____
: _____
: _____

TO-DO ... keep your soul on the agenda

1. _____
2. _____
3. _____
   _____
   _____
   _____

BODY & WELLNESS My body knows ...

DEVOTION Devotion creates miracles.

NOT WORKING ... don't hold back

STOP DOING ... clarity is power

GRATEFUL ... note WHY you're grateful   *Because ...*

FLOWING

You are a really good person and you deserve to be here.

THURSDAY December 26, 2019 | *Boxing Day (CAN, AUS) | Annular Solar Eclipse*

MY CORE DESIRED FEELINGS   *What I will do to feel the way I want to feel*

SCHEDULE ... work for Love

: _____
: _____
: _____
: _____
: _____
: _____
: _____
: _____
: _____
: _____
: _____
: _____
: _____
: _____
: _____

TO-DO ... make choices that liberate you

1. _____
2. _____
3. _____
   _____
   _____
   _____

BODY & WELLNESS I will tend to my body ...

DEVOTION I will contemplate ...

NOT WORKING ... claim it. Tame it.

STOP DOING ... don't take any crap

GRATEFUL ... be a beacon of optimism   *Because ...*

GRITTY

Trust your anger.

FRIDAY December 27, 2019

MY CORE DESIRED FEELINGS

What I will do to feel the way I want to feel

SCHEDULE ... simplicity is freedom

: _____
: _____
: _____
: _____
: _____
: _____
: _____
: _____
: _____
: _____
: _____
: _____
: _____
: _____
: _____
: _____
: _____

TO-DO ... imagine

1. _____
2. _____
3. _____
   _____
   _____
   _____

BODY & WELLNESS I will nourish my body ...

DEVOTION I will pray for (who/what) ...

NOT WORKING ... feel free

STOP DOING ... freedom is your birthright

GRATEFUL ... specificity intensifies gratitude

Because ...

Aim to get better at what you're already great at. THAT's mastery.

DAUNTLESS

SATURDAY December 28, 2019
Mercury enters Capricorn

MY CORE DESIRED FEELINGS

TO-DO ... visualize your ideal life

1. _____
2. _____
3. _____
   _____
   _____
   _____

REFLECT
Hands on your heart, eyes closed, recite your CDFs and see what images arise.

SUNDAY December 29, 2019

What I will do to feel the way I want to feel

TO-DO ... let it be easy

1. _____
2. _____
3. _____
   _____
   _____
   _____

ENVISION
What Core Desired Feeling(s) need extra attention this week?

SOUL PROMPT My superpower is

MASTERFUL

Respect your wishes.

MONDAY December 30, 2019 | *Chanukah/Hanukkah ends - evening (Jewish holiday)*

MY CORE DESIRED FEELINGS   *What I will do to feel the way I want to feel*

SCHEDULE ... does it light you up?

: _____
: _____
: _____
: _____
: _____
: _____
: _____
: _____
: _____
: _____
: _____
: _____
: _____
: _____
: _____
: _____

TO-DO ... prioritize pleasure

1. _____
2. _____
3. _____
   _____
   _____
   _____

BODY & WELLNESS My body helps me ...

DEVOTION My meditation will be ...

NOT WORKING ... does it feel light or heavy?

STOP DOING ... speak up

GRATEFUL ... ask for more   *Because ...*

Be a sanctuary.

NIRVANA

TUESDAY December 31, 2019 | *New Year's Eve*

MY CORE DESIRED FEELINGS

What I will do to feel the way I want to feel

SCHEDULE ... *joy expands time*

: _____
: _____
: _____
: _____
: _____
: _____
: _____
: _____
: _____
: _____
: _____
: _____
: _____
: _____
: _____
: _____
: _____

TO-DO ... *do what lights you up*

1. _____
2. _____
3. _____
   _____
   _____
   _____

BODY & WELLNESS *My body is ...*

DEVOTION *I will dedicate this day to ...*

NOT WORKING ... *name it so you can change it*

STOP DOING ... *No makes way for Yes*

GRATEFUL ... *gratitude puts everything into perspective*   *Because ...*

IN SYNC

Slow down if you need to, but don't ever stop.

IDEAS. DESIRES. WISDOM. ... your desires are sacred

RESILIENT

THE PAST MONTH: Reflect. Clarify. Create.

YOUR PLEASURE IS A FORM OF YOUR POWER.
Feeling good increases your flexibility, resiliency, effectiveness, and magnetism.

MY CORE DESIRED FEELINGS
My CDFs are strongest in… I feel most aligned with… I'm moving toward…
I want to give more attention to…

MY GOALS & INTENTIONS
My goals are bringing my CDFs to life… I need to change up, refine or deepen…
To move closer to my goals & intentions I…

WHAT'S REALLY WORKING, YA!
I really felt [your CDF] when… This month I was so brilliant…
I created… I felt… I allowed… I accomplished…

WHAT NEEDS TO SHIFT
I felt disappointed… The challenge…

THE NEW MONTH: Envision. Intend. Energize.

YOU ARE MADE OF LIGHT.
"Listen. / Every molecule is humming / its particular pitch. /
Of course you are a symphony. / Whose tune do you think /
the planets are singing / as they dance?"
— Lynn Ungar

HOW I WILL
be stronger… softer… more determined… less uptight… more flexible… less constricted… more open…
less accommodating… more accommodating… less worried… more generous… less doubtful…
more trusting… less punishing… more pleasure-creating… less fearful… more loving...

TO MOVE TOWARD MY GOALS & INTENTIONS…

IN THE SHOP

We have a gift for you!
25% OFF
your order!

Use code: **DMFRIENDS** in Danielle's Shop
This doesn't include Facilitator programs, we have another special offer for that below.

DANIELLELAPORTE.COM/SHOP

FACILITATOR PROGRAMS
Workshop, retreat, and coaching curriculum.

The Desire Map Facilitator Program

Coaching and workshop curriculum to guide people to discover their *Core Desired Feelings* and set goals with soul. Deepen the transformational work you're already doing with those you serve, or begin to serve in this new way.

The Fire Starter Sessions Facilitator Program

Business coaching and career development tools for helping your clients *define success on their own terms* and create a plan to make it happen.

Get $100 off your first year.

Use code: **FACILITATOR19** at checkout
when you purchase either license.

Photo: CatherineJust.com

Danielle LaPorte

...is the author of *White Hot Truth: Clarity for keeping it real on your spiritual path—from one seeker to another*, *The Fire Starter Sessions*, and *The Desire Map: A guide to creating goals with soul*—a book that has been translated into 12 languages, evolved into this yearly day planner and journal system, a Top 10 iTunes app, and an international workshop program with licensed facilitators in 15+ countries.

Danielle is an invited member of Oprah's *SuperSoul 100*. Named one of the "Top 100 Websites for Women" by *Forbes*, millions of visitors go to **DanielleLaPorte.com** monthly for her daily #Truthbombs and what's been called "the best place online for kickass spirituality." *Entrepreneur* magazine calls Danielle, "equal parts poet and entrepreneurial badass...edgy, contrarian... loving and inspired."

Her charities of choice are VDay: a global movement to end violence against women and girls, and Charity Water, setting out to bring safe drinking water to everyone in the world.

She lives in Vancouver, BC. You can find her **@daniellelaporte** and just about everywhere on social media.

The Day Planner cover art is by MARTA SPENDOWSKA

...a Polish-born, now New Hampshire Seacoast-based, American artist. Since 2007 Marta has worked with a wide range of art collectors, art consultants, fashion and beauty brands, and interior designers. Client roster includes *Oprah Magazine*, *NY Observer*, Danielle LaPorte, *Better Homes & Gardens*, Oreo and many more.

verymarta.com
@martaspendowska

Compassion is so often the solution